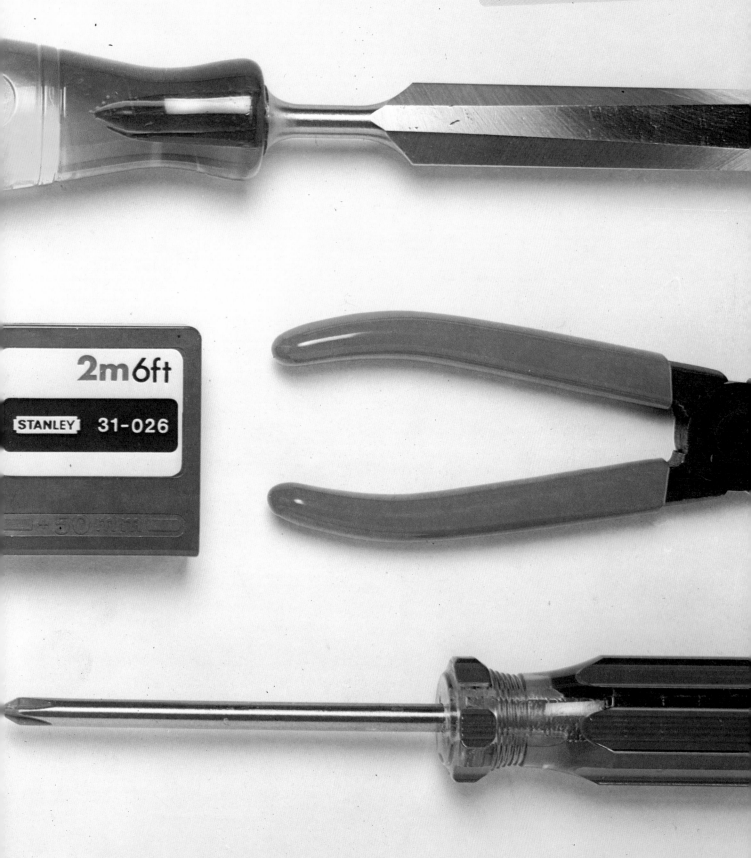

THE QUICK AND EASY GUIDE TO

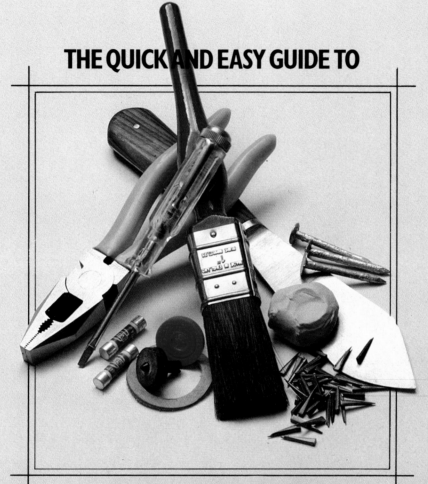

HOME REPAIRS

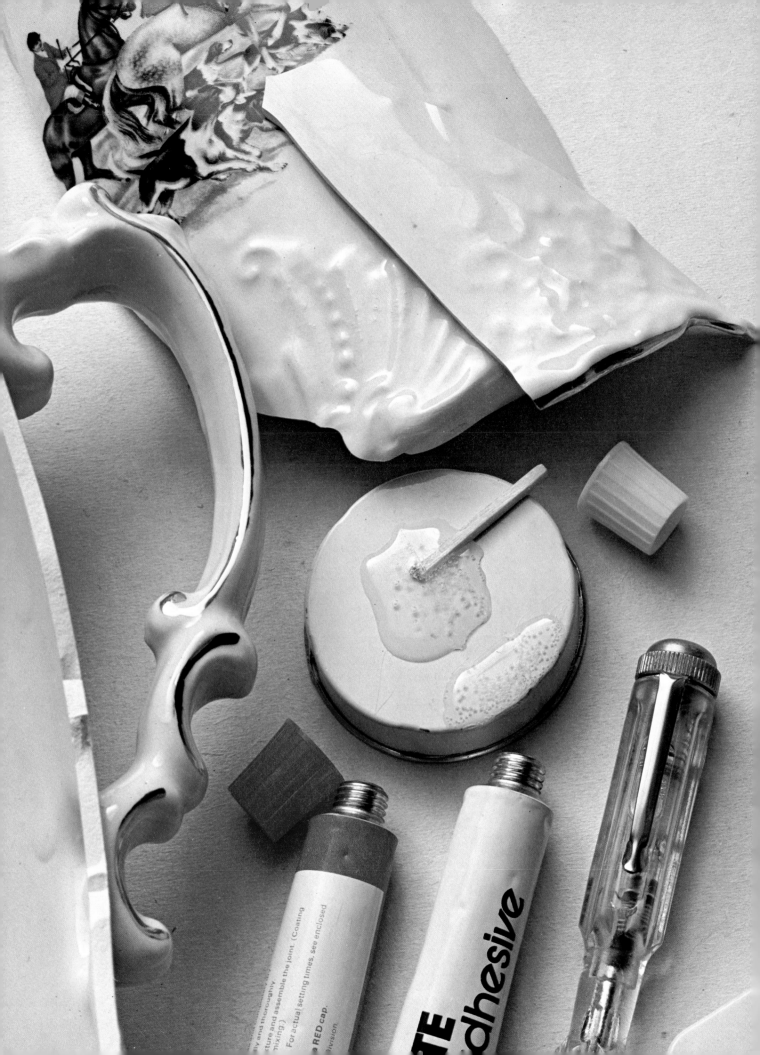

THE QUICK AND EASY GUIDE TO

HOME REPAIRS

RON GRACE

OCTOPUS

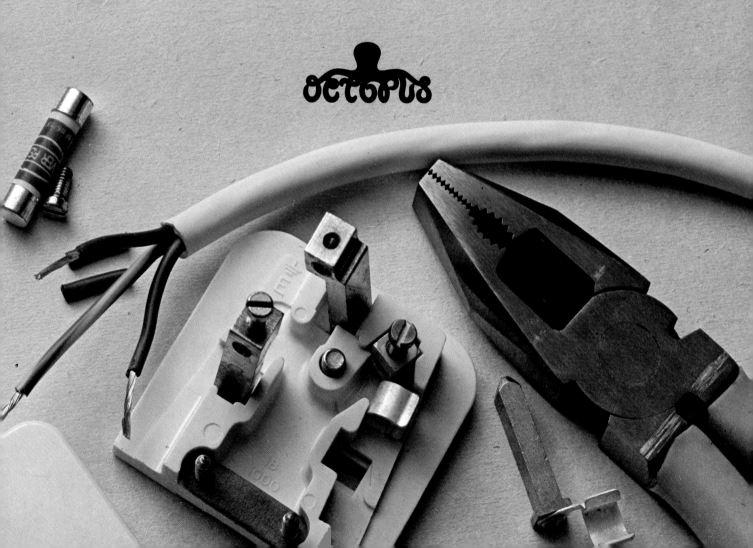

Contents

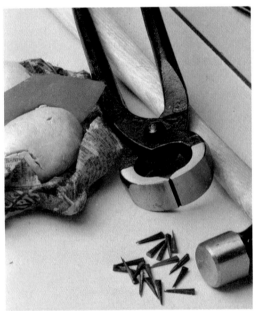

First published in 1979 by
Sundial Books Limited

This edition published in 1982 by
Octopus Books Limited
59 Grosvenor Street
London W1

©1979 Hennerwood Publications Limited

ISBN 0 7064 1780 1

Printed in Hong Kong

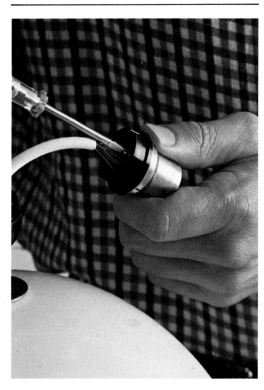

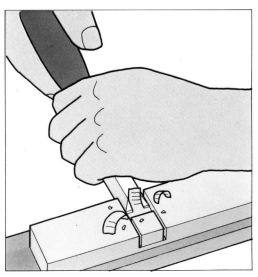

Introduction

Professional rates for doing quite minor home repairs have become exorbitant, yet many of these jobs could be tackled without difficulty by the average householder. *Home Repairs* is an invaluable handbook for every aspiring handyman or woman. It provides a comprehensive guide to all the systems and installations in your home, with full instructions on how to keep them in excellent working order.

The scope of home repairs is enormous — and certainly involves more than tightening up the occasional loose screw or knocking in a nail to hold up a sagging shelf. People who are quite unruffled about tiling a floor or papering a wall become very apprehensive at the thought of dealing with electrical repairs or plumbing. Although this initial hesitation is perfectly natural, remember that *Home Repairs* provides you with easy-to-follow instructions, and lots of step-by-step illustrations to help you as you work. As a further incentive, keep in mind the amount of money you can save.

The basic house structure, though apparently sound, is subject to constant wear and tear by the weather, settling of the foundations, and by physical damage. Accordingly, the section on repairs to major structures such as walls, ceilings, floors and roofs is extensive. Electrical repairs are clearly explained, and range from changing a worn plug to updating and extending your installations. Although plumbing seems very difficult, a little practice on simple jobs like changing tap washers and extending pipe runs will give you the confidence to go on to major projects such as kitchen and bathroom refits.

If you have problems such as damp, rot or beetle infestation, advice is provided on how to stop the trouble from spreading, and how to use preventative treatment. Outdoor jobs are also included, so you can repair paths, fences, gates and exterior walls.

Safety

Safety is a key feature in *Home Repairs*. Most safety precautions would seem to be a matter of common sense; however, it is well known that thousands of accidents take place in the home.. Before you start on any home repair, read quickly through this list of reminders:

When working on ladders, ensure that they are firmly secured, preferably at top and bottom. If the ground is uneven, use pieces of wood or other suitable material to support the stile not touching the ground. Always be careful to keep your weight well within the load-bearing area of the ladder. Take particular care when a ladder is resting on a plastic gutter.

Always use a proper roof ladder when working on a roof. A roof ladder has a large hook at the top which grips the ridge, giving a secure anchorage. When working on a roof it is best to have a tower scaffold for the vertical part of the climb. When using a ladder it is essential for it to be firmly secured at eaves level.

On a corrugated asbestos roof, always use a scaffold or other stout board on which to walk.

High shelves and tall cupboards may tempt you to stand on boxes, chairs or other unsteady supports — don't. Always keep a pair of kitchen steps handy where access is difficult.

Blowtorches are excellent tools for burning off paint, but do take extra care when working near flammable materials.

Sharp cutting tools not only produce good work, they also reduce the danger of accident. Blunt tools are frustrating for the user and require considerably more effort if they are to cut at all — and therein lies the danger.

When working with cutting tools, always keep your hands behind the cutting edge and work away from the body. Develop this technique as a habit; a moment's inattention could mean a hospital visit, or worse.

Power tools are fitted with safety guards by manufacturers; do not remove or interfere with them. When working on metal with power tools, clamp workpieces firmly. If a tool should snag on metalwork, the workpiece can spin at high speed and cause serious injury.

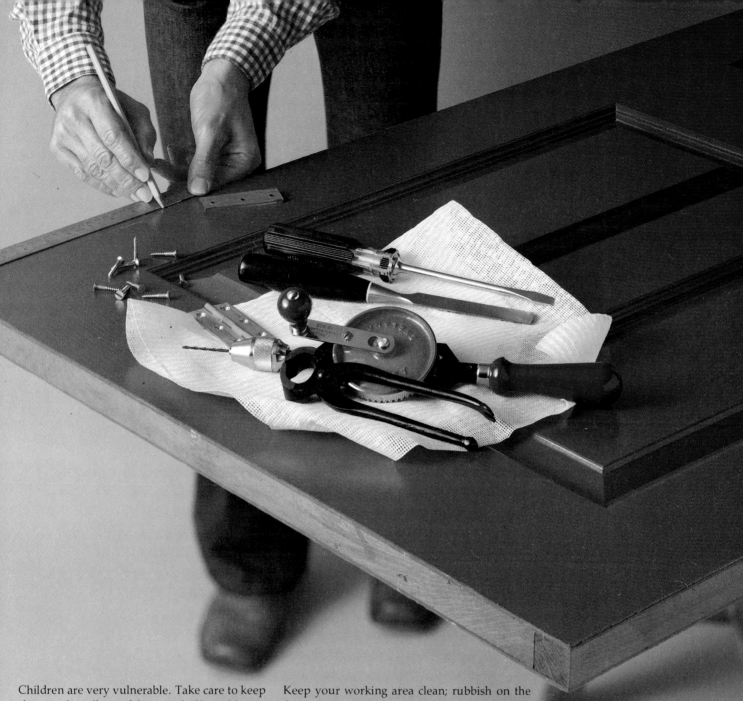

Children are very vulnerable. Take care to keep sharp tools well out of their reach. Hot soldering irons don't look hot, so they are even more dangerous — to you, too! Always unplug power tools when leaving them, even for a few minutes. And for your own safety, always unplug before changing bits, blades or other cutting attachments.

Never put such liquids as paint stripper or wood preservative into bottles or jars that could, just conceivably, be mistaken for a drink container. *Labelling will not do: young children cannot read.*

Take great care of your eyes; a pair of safety spectacles is an excellent investment. Use them when wire-brushing (hand or power), when using dangerous chemicals (such as paint stripper) and when using grinding and cutting discs on an electric power tool.

Keep your working area clean; rubbish on the floor can cause you to fall. When lifting floorboards or any work involving nails and screws in timber, don't leave the nails/screws sticking out where feet can tread on them.

Cleaners, solvents and some adhesives (which use petroleum based solvents) are flammable, so never use them in confined areas. Always open doors and windows to prevent a build-up of flammable vapour. Extinguish naked lights (pilot lights on gas appliances are easily forgotten) and, of course, don't smoke.

When working with asbestos, take particular care as this is extremely dangerous material. A breathing mask is cheap and will come in useful for a variety of dusty jobs. A handkerchief over the mouth is not good enough.

Interior repairs

There are two great advantages about doing interior repair jobs — they can be carried out at any time of the year regardless of the weather conditions, and the finished work is not affected by what the elements are doing afterwards.

One important reason for carrying out many interior repairs is appearance, and this is where you can make the best use of the time available. Whatever the weather, the work will be in exactly the same state when you resume as when you left it.

Many interior repair jobs are comparatively easy and, provided you take your time, the finished results will satisfy the most critical of observers — you!

The tools you will need are fairly basic and simple to use. If you should need something special for a particular job — such as a steam wallpaper stripper or heavy duty hammer drill — then remember that these can often be hired for a few days from your local hire shop. While a fairly substantial deposit will be required on expensive tools, the hire charges are quite reasonable and some shops even do half-day rates which can cut the cost even more.

Floor repairs

We usually do not notice the surfaces we walk on until they give trouble, and the two most common types of floor construction, timber and concrete, have their troubles from time to time.

Timber floors, which can be on any floor level, can creak, suffer from woodworm and other timber pest attacks, and be weakened by fungus troubles.

Concrete ground floors can suffer from cracks, holes, rising damp and condensation. These problems can be cured with simple, modern treatments.

All too often, timber floors are covered with carpets and vinyls, but with suitable treatment they can be made into decorative surfaces which take a lot of beating. There are many other jobs, too, which can be tackled, from refixing ceramic tiles to repairing carpets. Such jobs are well within your scope, so take a fresh look at the stuff under your feet.

Before starting on a job such as repairing a window, make sure that you assemble all the tools and equipment you will need. Pull back carpets to clear the area for working.

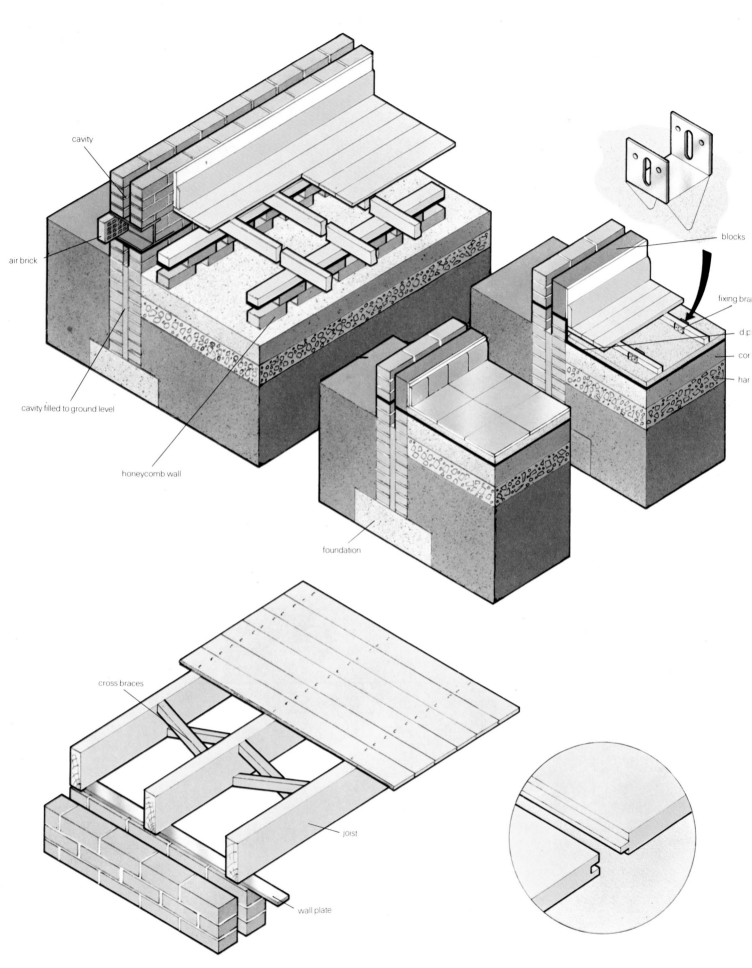

cavity

air brick

cavity filled to ground level

honeycomb wall

foundation

blocks

fixing bra

d.p

cor

har

cross braces

joist

wall plate

10

Solid floors are usually found only in ground floor rooms, except in purpose-built maisonettes and flats. With solid floors there will be no sign of air bricks in outer walls at floor level.

Timber floors are almost invariably found in upper rooms, and also at ground floor level in older houses. There will be air bricks in outer walls in this case.

Solid floor repairs

Damp surface A damp floor will ruin floorcoverings, cause smells, and loosen tiles and blocks. If a damp floor is suspected, try this rough and ready test. Lay a few vinyl floor tiles or sheets of vinyl floorcovering at random over the floor and leave for a few days. Moisture on the underside indicates that the floor is severely damp.

If the surface is otherwise sound, it will be sufficient to cure the dampness by treating the floor with a chemical waterproofing liquid or, more effectively, with a two-part epoxy emulsion paint, or a one-part moisture-curing polyurethane sealer. The latter two form a water-resistant barrier over which any floorcovering can be laid.

Each waterproofing treatment is supplied with full instructions, but requires a thoroughly cleaned floor. Remove skirting boards (see page 21) so the treatment can be taken up the walls to link with a damp-proof course.

The floor can be damp or dry at the time of application but the surface must be reasonably smooth. Fill hollows with cement mortar or treat the entire floor with a self-smoothing screed (see below). When the sealer is mixed and applied over the floor it provides a waterproof surface.

Smoothing an uneven surface An uneven solid floor is easy to smooth with a self-smoothing screed. The several makes of screeds can be applied over concrete, cement mortar, quarry tiles, ceramic tiles, flag stones, terrazzo, slate and bricks. Some types can be applied over vinyl tiles if these are securely fixed, and others are suitable for covering wood blocks if these are properly stuck down (see Repairing worn floorboards, page 13).

In most cases, self-smoothing screeds are applied in layers from 1½mm to 3mm (1/16in to 1/8in) thick, and two applications can be made. Hollows more than 6mm (¼in) deep must first be filled with cement mortar.

After scraping and sweeping the floor and washing it with strong sugar soap solution, paint the hollow with a pva bonding agent. Allow this coat to dry, apply another coat of bonding agent, and while this is wet fill the hollow with cement mortar. A suitable mix is one part Portland cement to three parts clean, coarse sand (parts are by volume).

Reasonably absorbent floor surfaces, such as concrete and cement mortar, are prepared for screeding by dampening with water.

Dusty surfaces and non-absorbent floors, like quarry tiles, should be primed with a bonding agent, as mentioned above, or with a special acrylic primer. The latter is suitable for priming vinyl floor tiles if these are to be covered with a screed. They must be securely stuck down.

Most screeding compounds are supplied in powder form and are made ready for use by mixing with water to form a creamy paste. Pour a little on the floor, starting in the corner farthest from the door, and spread it as evenly as

LEFT: *Floor construction in a typical cavity wall house. A variety of solid ground floor constructions is shown* **(Top)**, *also the arrangement at first floor level* **(Bottom)**.

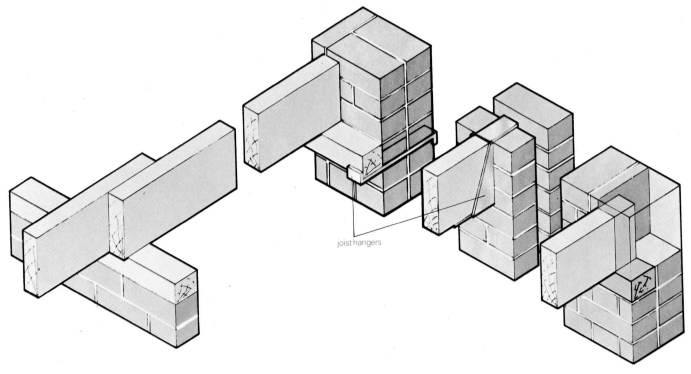

joist hangers

possible to the thickness required, using a steel float. The screed settles to a smooth finish, float marks disappearing within a few minutes.

The screed can usually be walked on in about two hours. At this stage a second coat can be applied if necessary. Floorcoverings can be laid the next day, although maximum hardness is not attained for a week.

Replacing damaged quarry tiles If damage is widespread, resurface the floor with a self-smoothing screed (see above). An isolated broken tile can be removed and replaced.

Wearing safety spectacles, use a hammer and chisel to break up the damaged tile (see diagram 1) so it can be removed piece by piece without loosening adjacent tiles. Use a cold chisel to clean up the hole. Put the new tile in place to check that it will rest with its surface level with, or just below, the surrounding tiles. Remove the tile, spread a layer of ceramic floor tiling adhesive on the cleared surface (see diagram 2), take the new tile and press it into position. Scrape off surplus adhesive with a trowel (see diagram 3). After 24 hours, grout with a cement mix consisting of one part Portland cement to four parts clean, coarse sand. Rub the cement mix into the joints, using a rag, and sponge away the surplus while it is still wet.

Refixing a loose ceramic tile Lift the loose tile and chip off the old grouting from its edges. Check that the tile is flush with the surrounding

When replacing a damaged quarry tile, wear safety spectacles at all times.
1. *Break up the damaged tile with a hammer and chisel, and remove pieces with a small cold chisel.*
2. *Spread a layer of ceramic floor tiling adhesive in the hole.*
3. *Press the new tile firmly into position, scrape off any surplus adhesive with a trowel.*

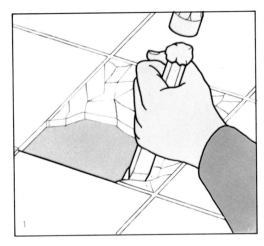

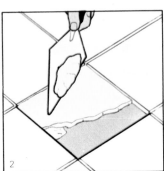

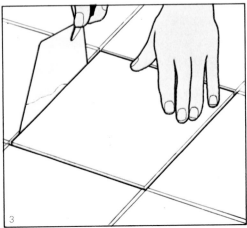

floor surface when it is replaced. Lift it again and spread ceramic floor tile adhesive on its underside. Press the tile into position, checking it is level with the surrounding surface, and grout as described above.

Timber Floor Repairs

Lifting floorboards Access to underfloor space is essential for many jobs. In most cases there will be an access point where, for example, the electrical equipment has been installed, and raising floorboards will be fairly easy: insert a floorboard bolster at the joint between the two halves of the board and lever upwards. When sufficient leverage has been gained a claw hammer can be used (see diagram 4) to raise the board high enough to insert a suitable pivot, such as a piece of broom handle. At this point, downward pressure at the cut end will force up the remaining part of the board.

The nails may be left in the board or in the joists, and in either case they can be removed with a claw hammer, straightened, and reused.

If the board will not lift easily screws, not nails, may be holding the board down. A previously unlifted board may be of the tongued and grooved type, and the tongue will have to be cut through on either side of the board (see diagram 5). This can be done with a convex blade floorboard saw or with a circular saw set to cut a little less than the thickness of the board. If the depth is set correctly (20mm/¾in), there will be no risk of damage to joists or contact with underlying electrical cables. For complete safety, if in any doubt, turn off the electrical supply at the mains and saw by hand.

It may be necessary to lift a board which runs in a continuous length from one side of the room to the other. The easiest way is to make the necessary cut with an electric jig saw across the board close to one of the joists.

A circular saw can also be used although it will cut into the boards on either side of the one being worked on. An alternative method is to drill a hole in the board and use a pad saw to cut across.

The line of the joist can be determined by the row of nails holding the boards down. For an accurate location of the edge of the joist, slide an ordinary razor blade between the boards until it touches the edge of the joist.

Chipboard flooring poses a more difficult problem. Cut out a panel or, for tongued and grooved chipboard sheets, cut through the tongues all around a panel before levering up the complete sheet.

After cutting a board, the end will need support when it is replaced. Support the cut end with a scrap of 25mm × 50mm (1in × 2in) timber nailed to the side of the joist (see diagram 6). Screw, do not nail, the joist end down, as screws will not displace the piece of supporting timber.

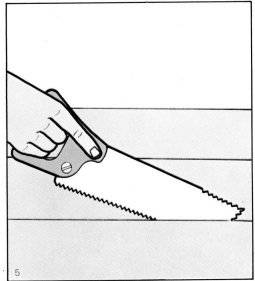

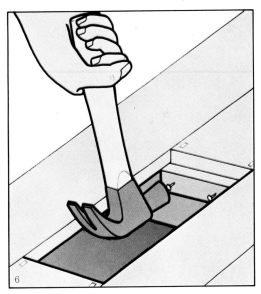

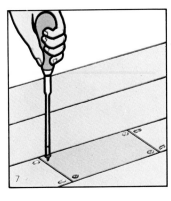

Repairing worn floorboards A simple and often effective cure is to lift the affected boards and then refix them upside down.

If only a few boards are worn it may be better to replace these with new floorboards.

If the entire floor is affected it can be levelled with a floor sanding machine which leaves a new surface suitable for treatment with a wood sealer and used as a decorative feature. Where the boards are to be covered with a wall-to-wall floorcovering, the floor can be levelled with a special latex screeding compound or sheets of hardboard.

A floor sanding machine (available from hire shops), will take about 3mm (⅛in) off the surface in a short time. The first stage is to drive nail heads below the surface using a nail punch and hammer. A sheet of abrasive cloth is fixed to the sanding drum of the sanding machine. A powerful electric motor turns the drum at high speed. The sander is moved backwards and forwards in the direction of the run of the floorboards or at a slight angle to them.

For the first few passes, medium or coarse grade abrasive cloth is used, but the last few runs are made with the fine grade. The machines have dust extraction bags, but it is still a dusty and noisy job.

If the floor is to be levelled with a latex screed, it is first scraped free of loose and flaking materials and swept clean. Grease, paint or old adhesive should be removed. Loose boards must be refixed (see below).

Latex screed, which may be bought as a powder to be mixed with water or as a two-part compound incorporating powder and liquid, is self-smoothing and trowel marks disappear in a short time. The floor can be walked on in one to four hours, the floorcovering can be laid the next day, and maximum hardness is achieved in a week. The screed forms a pliable but tough covering.

Another way to resurface a timber floor is to use hardboard sheets. Usually 3.2mm (⅛in) thick standard hardboard is suitable, but use 4.8mm (³/₁₆in) thick board if the floor is very uneven or there are gaps more than about 5mm (³/₁₆in) wide between the floorboards. Lay tempered hardboard, which is water resistant, in kitchens, bathrooms, or any rooms where there could be dampness.

Before it is laid, the hardboard must be conditioned to stop it from buckling at a later date. Normally it is sufficient to separate the boards and stand them on edge for 72 hours in the room where they are to be laid.

The boards must be conditioned with water if they are to be laid in new houses, kitchens or bathrooms, where there could be moisture on the floor. Each 2,440 × 1,220mm (8/4ft) sheet will need about ½ litre (1 pint) of water sprinkled over the rough mesh side of the hardboard. Stack the boards back to back on a flat surface; leave standard boards for 48 hours, and tempered boards for 72 hours.

4. *To lift a floorboard, insert a floorboard bolster and lever upwards with a claw hammer.*
5. *To cut through a tongue and groove type floorboard, saw through on either side of the board.*
6. *A cut board will need to be supported when replaced. Nail a small piece of timber to the side of the joist.*
7. *When access to the pipes is necessary, leave screwed down access panels.*

The hardboard is laid as soon as it is conditioned. Lay it mesh side up unless it is to be covered with thin vinyl floor tiles. Cutting the sheets into 1,220mm (4ft) squares makes them easier to handle. Nail them down using 20mm to 25mm (¾in to 1in) rust-resistant ring shank nails or hardboard pins spaced at 150mm (6in) intervals overall, and at 100mm (4in) intervals around the edge. Where access to pipes is necessary, leave screwed down access panels (see diagram 7).

Repairing damaged floorboards Lift the damaged board by easing it up with a bolster chisel inserted near the end of the board. If the floor has tongued and grooved boards it will first be necessary to cut along the tongue by sawing along one side of the board with a pad saw or electric jig saw. Cut out the damaged section so that the end of the remaining length of board falls half-way across a joist. Fit the new section so its ends neatly coincide with the mid points of joists.

Fixing loose floorboards In many cases renailing is sufficient, but first lift one or two boards to be certain that pipes and cables do not run close to the surface. Look for the old nail holes which indicate the run of the joists and insert the new nails (50mm/2in floor brads) so they will enter the joists, but slightly to one side of the old holes.

If the nail holes are enlarged or the ends of the boards have been split by frequent nailing, screw down the boards using 38mm (1½in) gauge 10 countersunk head wood screws.

If the boards still bounce after they have been refixed, the problem is probably in the joists themselves. The ends, which are either built into the walls or supported on metal brackets called joist hangers, may have rotted.

Lift a few boards so the joist ends can be inspected. If they have rotted, call in a timber preservation specialist; if there is dry rot, a new damp-proof course will be required.

If the joists are sound, but loose in their supports, they may be wedged with pieces of timber or supported on scraps of slates. Alternatively the joist ends can be fixed with new galvanised steel joist hangers, available from builders' merchants, which are cemented into mortar joints in the wall, or screwed to the wall with stout zinc-plated screws fitted into wall plugs.

Curing squeaking boards Dust talcum powder or French chalk into the crack between the affected boards. Make sure the boards are securely fixed. If the trouble recurs, lift the boards and plane the edges to give slight clearance. Refix the boards with screws.

If the treads of stairs creak, work pva glue into the joint between the tread and the lower riser, then drive screws through the tread and into the riser (see diagram 8).

If the underside of the staircase is accessible, reglue the wedges under the treads and risers, then drive the wedges fully home (see diagram 9). Add triangular blocks at the junctions of treads and risers and glue and screw the blocks in place (see diagram 10).

Curing excessive bounce in a floor If the bounce is near the side of the room see the section above on Fixing loose boards.

If the bounce is near the middle of the room the trouble could be due to the joists being fitted across an excessive span. Lift floorboards around the mid-point of the room and fit a line of struts between the joists (see diagram 11). The easiest to fit are lengths of floorboard about 125mm × 25mm (5in × 1in), glued and nailed between the joists.

Renovating a parquet or wood strip floor First cut out damaged blocks using a mallet and sharp chisel. Work from the middle of each block towards its edge. Scrape out old adhesive from the hole and cut new blocks, bought from a d-i-y shop or timber merchant, to fit. Glue these blocks in place with a suitable timber-flooring adhesive.

Sand the floor flat using a floor sanding machine (see Repairing worn floorboards, page 13). Afterwards, vacuum clean the floor and wipe it over with a damp cloth. Allow the surface to dry. The colour of the wood can then be brought up by applying an oleo-resinous sealer, or a polyurethane varnish. These sealers will also protect the surface from staining and scratching, and will need only a wipe over with a damp cloth from time to time.

Floorcovering repairs

Patching a carpet With hessian-backed carpets, turn the carpet over and mark the square to be removed. Paint around the cutting line with latex carpet adhesive and rub it well into the backing to prevent fraying when the square is removed. Put a scrap of wood under the damaged area and cut through the backing with a sharp trimming knife.

On a carpet remnant, or a part permanently covered by furniture, cut out a replacement piece making sure the pattern and pile direction closely matches the surrounding carpet. Cut the patch from the back of the remnant.

Cut strips of hessian to lay across the hole in the carpet, or around its perimeter if the hole is a large one. Coat the hessian strips with adhesive and stick them over the back of the hole. This forms a base upon which to glue the patch. Turn the carpet the right way up. Spread adhesive over the back of the patch and around its edges to prevent fraying. Press the patch into place and lightly hammer it down.

The technique for patching a foam-backed carpet is similar, but the damaged area and the replacement piece must be cut from the front of

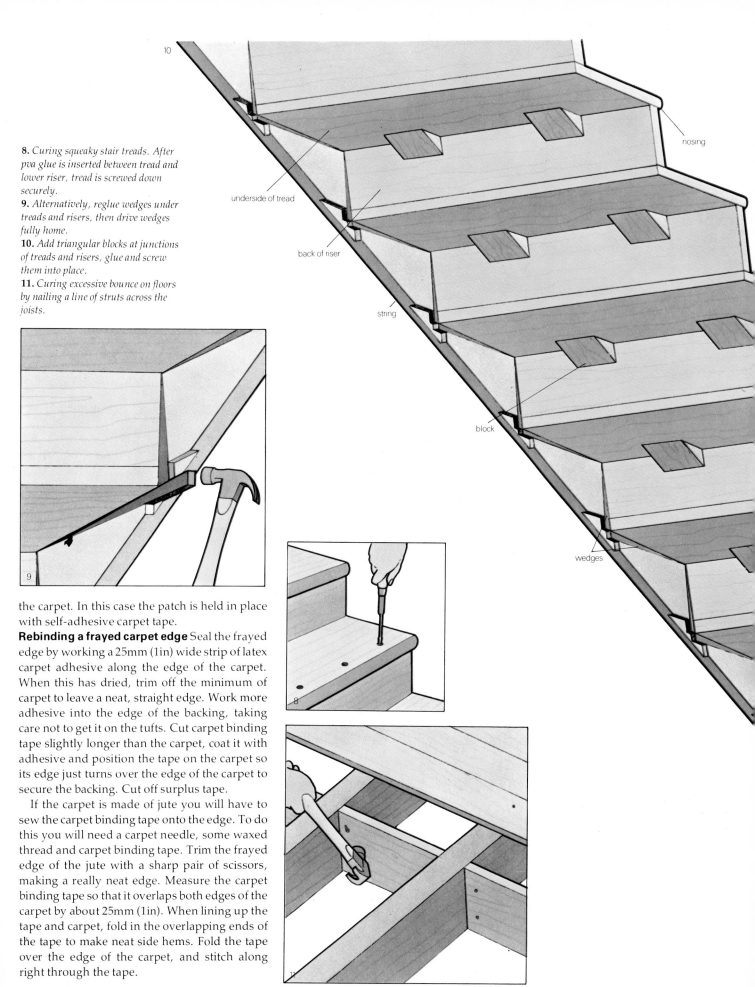

8. *Curing squeaky stair treads. After pva glue is inserted between tread and lower riser, tread is screwed down securely.*

9. *Alternatively, reglue wedges under treads and risers, then drive wedges fully home.*

10. *Add triangular blocks at junctions of treads and risers, glue and screw them into place.*

11. *Curing excessive bounce on floors by nailing a line of struts across the joists.*

nosing

underside of tread

back of riser

string

block

wedges

the carpet. In this case the patch is held in place with self-adhesive carpet tape.

Rebinding a frayed carpet edge Seal the frayed edge by working a 25mm (1in) wide strip of latex carpet adhesive along the edge of the carpet. When this has dried, trim off the minimum of carpet to leave a neat, straight edge. Work more adhesive into the edge of the backing, taking care not to get it on the tufts. Cut carpet binding tape slightly longer than the carpet, coat it with adhesive and position the tape on the carpet so its edge just turns over the edge of the carpet to secure the backing. Cut off surplus tape.

If the carpet is made of jute you will have to sew the carpet binding tape onto the edge. To do this you will need a carpet needle, some waxed thread and carpet binding tape. Trim the frayed edge of the jute with a sharp pair of scissors, making a really neat edge. Measure the carpet binding tape so that it overlaps both edges of the carpet by about 25mm (1in). When lining up the tape and carpet, fold in the overlapping ends of the tape to make neat side hems. Fold the tape over the edge of the carpet, and stitch along right through the tape.

Ceilings

House construction is a pretty conventional father-to-son sort of business and methods change very gradually, with the result that the old-fashioned lath-and-plaster ceilings (and walls) lasted for a very long time and modern plasterboard took a long time to become accepted. Thus it is not possible to say that, after a certain date, all ceilings are plasterboard.

When trouble strikes, perhaps in the shape of a bulge in a ceiling, the natural reaction is to call in the local plasterer, but there are repairs that can be carried out by the amateur, ways of hiding cracks and bulges and, in the extreme, it is quite possible to replace a whole ceiling, although it is a very messy job. But then it would be messy with a craftsman doing it.

Don't be put off by lurid 'over-a-pint' stories about plastering. Modern methods and materials, as in so many other fields, make the jobs much easier for the amateur. Have a go, and surprise yourself.

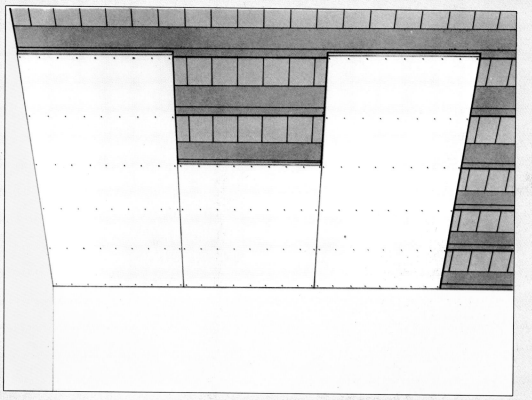

OPPOSITE: *A bulge in a lath and plaster ceiling can sometimes be persuaded into place using a flat board and a timber prop. Final fixing is done either with plaster or screws.*
LEFT: *A complete ceiling is covered with plasterboard exactly spanning the joists and with the end joints staggered.*
BELOW: *These basic tools and materials are required for ceiling repairs. You need water, plaster, a trowel, hawk, scrim, also wood and metal floats.*

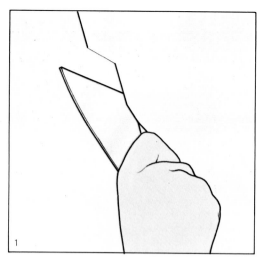

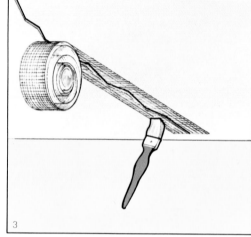

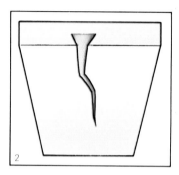

1. *Use the corner of a stripping knife to clean out hairline cracks, and form a V shaped cavity as shown in the insert* **2. (Left)**.
3. *Plasterboard cracks are filled using scrim to cover the surface and provide a bond.*

Repairing cracks

Hairline cracks Use a sharp knife to undercut the crack, (*see diagram 1*) scoring through the crack to leave a V-shaped cavity in the plaster (*see diagram 2*). The point of the V will be on the inner surface. Dust out the cavity.

Refill with a cellulose filler forced into the crack with a flexible filling knife. Finally, draw the knife across the surface to leave a flush finish. Alternatively, leave the filler proud of the surface and, when it has hardened, rub it smooth with glasspaper wrapped around a wooden or cork block.

Reopened cracks Cracks that reopen need a reinforced repair. Fill the crack as above and, using wallpaper paste as adhesive, fix a length of scrim mesh across the repair (*see diagram 3*). Cover the scrim with lining paper also fixed with wallpaper adhesive. The paper should be about 300mm (12in) wide and only the central portion should be pasted — sufficient to cover the scrim with a small margin on either side. When dry, carefully tear off the hanging paper to leave a fine, feathered edge on the ceiling. If necessary, brush a little filler over the edges.

Those cracks that continually re-open along the join of the ceiling to wall are due to normal house movement. Repairs can often be made using the scrim and lining paper method.

Where cracks open at different points it is possible to conceal the damage (and future cracks) by fixing cove around the room. Bought in standard lengths, cove is fixed with a special adhesive supplied by the manufacturers. Full fixing details are given with the cove.

Cracks in existing cove Cracks that develop in cove plastered in when the house was built can be filled with cellulose filler.

Should a major fault have left a large hole, fill it with a plaster such as sirapite applied by trowel. If there is difficulty in obtaining a smooth finish, smooth the plaster with glasspaper wrapped around a sponge; the sponge will form itself readily to the required contour.

The alternative is to fill the bulk of the hole with plaster and allow it to set. Complete the last 6mm (¼in) or so with filler, rubbed smooth when set. Shape with a wooden shape of the same profile.

Shop-bought lengths of cove do not usually match, in profile or width, original cove plastered into the house. They can, however, be used as a base for repair where a section of cove is missing, assuming that the shop-bought piece is shallower in profile and not wider than the existing cove.

Cut the new piece to size and fit it in the space, following manufacturer's instructions. To finish, build up the required profile using plaster or filler as previously detailed. Be sure to fill gaps between old and new cove before redecorating.

Repairing larger holes

Large holes in plasterboard Gain access to the ceiling from above, either from the loft or by lifting the floorboards in the room above. Cut a sheet of expanded metal mesh, larger than the hole, and fix it to the back of the plasterboard using blobs of filler to secure the edges (*see diagram 4*). Allow the filler to set, then complete the repair from the room side of the board. Use plaster, or plaster and filler, to fill the hole (see Cracks in existing cove, above).

Major damage entails inserting a new piece of plasterboard of the same thickness as the existing material. Cut around the damaged area using a sharp knife, and align the edges of the cut-out portion with the centre line of the joists above.

To ascertain the positions of joists, drill a couple of holes through the board from above on either side of the joists.

Cut out a piece of plasterboard to match the hole exactly. To cut, score with a sharp knife through the paper side of the board; bend it slightly, then complete the cut from the reverse face. Clean up the cut edges with a file or Surform.

To fix the board, hammer clout nails through

the edges, at 150mm (6in) intervals, going through into the joists (*see diagram 5*). The nails must be long enough to be well bedded in the joists. Drive their heads well into the surface and make good the slight depressions, using a filler.

To strengthen the joints around the repair, use the scrim and lining paper method described under Reopened cracks.

If a piece of plasterboard of the correct thickness is not obtainable, select a slightly thinner piece. Fix a framework of battens to the joists leaving their edges sufficiently proud of the joists to compensate for the thinner plasterboard (*see diagram 6*).

If the positions of the battens have been carefully calculated, when the plasterboard is fixed, a flush finish should be left. Make good joints and nail head holes as before.

Alternatively fix the thinner piece of plasterboard directly to the joists and make up the difference in levels with a skim coat of plaster.

Lath and plaster — large holes A bulge in the ceiling is caused by the plaster breaking away from the laths. It is sometimes possible to push the bulge back into place (using a length of timber) and insert rustless screws through into the laths to hold it in place. Sink the screw heads below surface and fill the holes with filler.

Should the screws crack the plaster, nothing is lost since the alternative is to remove the loose plaster and insert new plasterboard.

Cut out the damaged area from the ceiling, squaring up the sides of the cut with the joists above the laths. Hammer home any nails protruding from the laths.

If a piece of plasterboard equal in thickness to the existing plaster can be found, it can be cut out and fitted as for plasterboard repairs. Alternatively, select a thinner piece of board and make up the difference by fixing thin battens to the laths using panel pins. Cut and fix the plasterboard to the joists as described earlier.

A new ceiling

All modern ceilings are made by nailing plasterboard directly to the joists (*see diagram on page 17*). The lath and plaster method is obsolete.

It is well within the scope of the handyman to fix a new ceiling. The job is worth considering where, for example, an old lath and plaster ceiling is bulging in many places.

Removing the existing ceiling leads to a good deal of mess, especially with a lath and plaster type. Always wear protective glasses. If the loft is above the ceiling, the plaster and laths can be knocked out from above, and nails left in the joists can then be pulled out from below.

With a bedroom above the ceiling, the complete demolition should take place from below. Having hammered strategic holes in the plaster, the laths and nails can be removed with a claw hammer.

For joists spaced 400mm (16in) apart, use 9.5mm (³⁄₈in) thick plasterboard for the new ceiling. For joists spaced at intervals greater than 400mm (16in), use 12.7mm (½in) thick board. Plasterboard can be cut through the outer covering on one side and the board snapped over a sharp corner. Shapes can be formed accurately if a template is made of brown paper, and cut edges smoothed with a Surform tool or glasspaper.

The boards are nailed at right angles to the joists. Stagger the joints and arrange for all board edges to coincide with the centre line of the joists to allow for nail fixing points.

Joints should be strengthened with scrim and lining paper as described under Reopened cracks, and nail head holes filled with filler before the ceiling is finished off.

Finish with a skim coat of plaster, a textured compound ceiling effect or hang lining paper and decorate.

4. *When filling a large hole in plasterboard, expanded metal mesh can form a backing for the filler.*
5. *A patch which spans the joists makes a neat, easily concealed repair.*
6. *Where the old plaster thickness cannot be matched, a framework of battens fixed to the joists with panel pins will compensate. Nail the side battens to the joists first, and tack cross battens on their ends.*

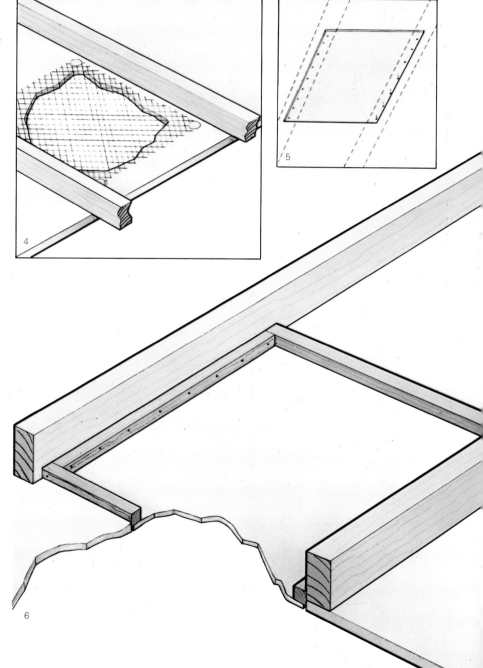

Interior walls

Interior walls are subject to much closer scrutiny than exterior ones and require a better finish. The likely causes of troubles are very much the same — settlement of the walls causes cracks in the plaster, and damp, whether penetrating from the outside or caused by condensation on the inside, can play havoc with decorations. Small children generally use their tiny fingers to change the overall appearance of wallcoverings.

Much can be done to correct damage without extensive redecoration work, and cover-up operations can be used until major redecorating is convenient.

There are many ways to improve the appearance of walls which, at first sight, may seem difficult, such as replacing old skirting boards. These jobs are just a matter of time and patience.

Repairing wallcoverings

Peeling wallcoverings Lift back the peeled section and apply some wallpaper paste with a small brush (*see diagram 1*). Press wallcovering back in place by rolling with a seam roller (*see diagram 2*). Wipe adhesive off with a damp cloth.

Torn wallpaper Using spare wallpaper match the pattern and prepare a patch with a ragged edge slightly larger than the damaged piece. When preparing the patch, tear the surplus away from the front of the patch so that the white backing paper does not show around the edge of the patch.

Turn the patch over and peel away some of the backing paper to form a feathered edge all around the patch. If the paper does not peel, rub sandpaper on the back of the patch to form a feathered edge. This will effectively disguise the patch.

Make sure there is no loose paper around the damaged area on the wall. Paste the patch and stick it in place, being careful to match the pattern. Roll down from the middle outwards, being especially careful to flatten the edges.

Torn vinyl and special wallcoverings Vinyls, hessians, grass cloths, flocks and other wallcoverings which will not tear must be repaired by cutting a patch to fit. This type of straight-edged patch is likely to be more noticeable than a torn feathered-edged patch.

Cut a spare piece of wallcovering to match the pattern and cover the damaged area. Hold the patch over the wallcovering so the patterns match and with a straight-edge guide cut through both patch and wallcovering with a sharp trimming knife (*see diagram 3*). This will ensure that the patch fits the hole perfectly. Remove all pieces of wallcovering from the damaged area (*see diagram 4*) and paste the patch in their place, lightly rolling it down (*see diagram 2*). A clean paint roller is ideal for this.

Bubbles The most satisfactory repair is to inject bubbles (*see diagram 5*) with wallpaper paste using a hypodermic syringe, available from chemists. After injecting the bubble, give the adhesive time to soak into the paper, then use a seam roller to flatten the paper. Work from the outer edge towards the middle. Paste that exudes through the needle hole must be wiped off with a damp cloth.

An alternative way to deal with bubbles is to slit the paper vertically and horizontally through the bubble. If possible, make the cuts along pattern lines where they will be less noticeable. Fold back the flaps (*see diagram 6*), apply wallpaper paste and allow it to soak in, then brush the flaps back into position and lightly roll down. Wipe away surplus adhesive.

Replacing ceramic tiles

Work a pointed scraper all around the damaged tile to remove the grouting. Wear protective glasses and working from the middle to the edges, use a hammer and small cold chisel to remove the damaged tile piece by piece. Do not try to prise it up from the edges or the surrounding tiles will be loosened. Clear adhesive from the plaster or cement mortar under the tiles and repair the surface with filler if necessary.

If a matching tile is not available, replace it with a toning or contrasting tile of the right shape and size. Change a few other tiles with similar replacements to build up a random pattern so that repairs will not be noticeable.

Spread tile adhesive on the back of the replacement tile and press it into place until its surface is aligned with the surrounding tiles. After 24 hours fill the gaps between the tiles with grouting. Wipe off the surplus and when dry polish the tiles with a duster.

If the damaged tile was mounted on a thick bed of loosened cement mortar, this must be chipped out. Brush some diluted pva bonding agent on the wall and the back of the replacement tile. While this is still tacky, apply cement mortar consisting of one part Portland cement to three parts clean coarse sand mixed to the right consistency with equal parts of pva bonding agent and water. Press the replacement tile into place so it is level with the other tiles. Grout the joints after 48 hours.

Repairing skirting boards
Repairing a damaged section of skirting board
The skirting is fixed to the walls with nails, so remove it by levering away from the wall (*see diagram 7*). Car tyre levers are useful for this job, but protect the wall with scraps of wood.

When the board is free, the damaged part can

1. *When seams lift, use a small brush to persuade a little paste under the edge.*

2. *Use a seam roller to flatten the edges. Do not roll heavily on embossed wallcoverings.*

3. *Patching. Lay the new piece over the old, matching patterns, and cut through both layers.*

4. *Pull the cut portion away from the wall. The new piece will fit the cut-out exactly.*

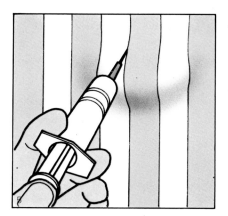

5. *Bubbles can often be cured by injecting paste with a hypodermic syringe.*

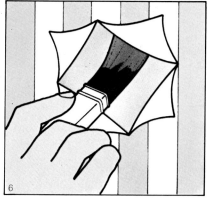

6. *For bubbles which cannot be injected, cut flaps, apply paste and smooth back into position.*

OPPOSITE: *Three kinds of partition walls, constructed in brick, block and timber and plasterboard.*

be cut away and a new section inserted, or the entire length can be replaced. New skirting boards should be the same depth as the old ones to avoid replastering; the plaster is rarely taken far below the top of the skirtings.

If the damaged part only is to be removed, make 45 degree mitre cuts on each side of the damaged area (*see diagram 8*). Make matching cuts on each end of the new piece of skirting. Glue and screw pieces of timber, no more than plaster thick, behind the mitre cuts so they overlap the joints. Glue and screw the replacement section in place (*see diagram 9*).

It is a good idea to paint the back of the skirting with wood preservative before fixing it to the wall. The skirting may be fixed to timber blocks, called grounds, which are nailed to the surface of the wall, or it may be fixed to timber wedges, or plugs, which are inserted into gaps between bricks.

Damaged grounds are easily replaced (*see diagram 10*). They can be fixed with masonry pins, which are driven into the wall, or with screws driven into wall plugs.

Damaged wedges are harder to replace. To remove them, partially insert a large screw which can be gripped with a claw hammer or pincers. New wedges are prepared to the shape shown (*see diagram 11*). The twist makes the wedge anchor firmly between the bricks when it is driven home. Both wedges and grounds should be treated with wood preservative before they are fitted.

Replacing a length of skirting board When an entire length of skirting is replaced, the new board must be shaped to fit at each end. If the skirting terminates in an external angle, cut the end of the board to a 45 degree mitre. When the end is an internal angle, mark the profile shape of the skirting on the face side or back of the new

board (*see diagram 13*). Carefully cut along this line with a coping saw. The skirting will now fit neatly against a square cut board.

Picture rails

Refixing a picture rail Picture rails are usually nailed to walls with 64mm (2½in) cut nails. If the rail is loose, refix with these nails, or use the same length masonry nails. Insert the nails at a slight downward angle and drive the nail heads just below the surface using a nail punch. Put a blob of paint on the nail head to prevent rusting, and fill the dent with wood filler.

Removing a picture rail Think carefully before removing a picture rail. The trend is to restore houses to their original condition. If rails are removed you will have to fill holes left by the securing nails, remove accumulations of paint and wallpaper which could show as a ridge, and even try to make good an uneven thickness of plaster above and below the rail.

To remove a rail with the least damage to a wall, start in the middle of a long length of rail. Lever the rail away from the wall until a scrap of board can be placed between the rail and the wall. Saw through the rail, with the board protecting the wall. The section of rail will now be easy to remove. Remove accumulated paint and wallpaper with a blowlamp. Fill holes in plaster as described below.

Paint troubles on walls

Flaking paint This is caused by poor surface preparation. Scrape away all traces of peeling paint. Wash the surface with warm water and sugar soap solution and rinse with clean water. Allow the surface to dry then rub down with abrasive paper. Wipe over with a damp sponge. Rub the surface with a clean hand for signs of chalkiness, which may occur if distemper has

Replacing a length of damaged skirting board.

7. *Levering the damaged skirting board away from the wall. A pad of wood is used to prevent damage.*

8. *Cutting the replacement piece of board on a workmate. A 45 degree cut matches that on the old board.*

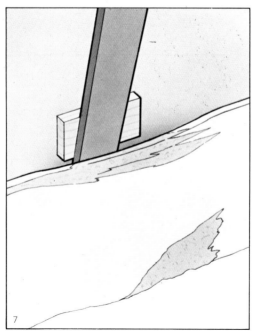

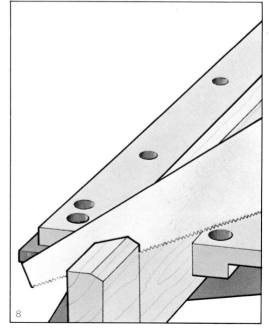

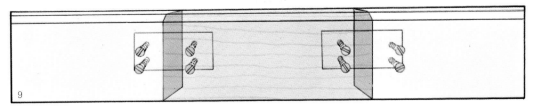

9. *The new section of board is fitted in place with mitres at each end.*
10. *Grounds are fixed to the face of the wall to support the skirting board.*
11. *Cut a skew wedge which fits between the bricks.*
12. *Hammering the skew wedge home in the mortar joint space.*
13. *Mitres do not have to be made at corners. Here the boards are scribed to match each other.*

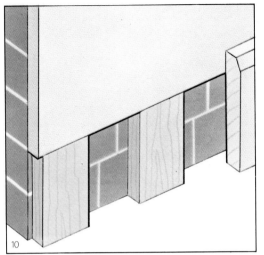

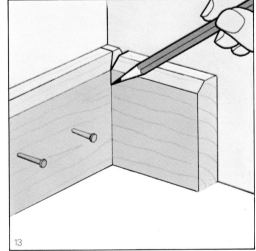

been applied to the wall. In this case paint the wall with a stabilising solution before repainting.

Chipped paint Rub down the area with medium abrasive paper. Make sure the paint at the edge of the chip is secure. Fill the depression with fine surface filler. When dry, flatten the surface with fine grade abrasive paper before touching in with new paint.

Blistered paint This may occur on gloss painted walls, particularly if the wall is damp, or it may be due to poor surface preparation. Rub down to a sound surface. Fill depressions with fine surface wall filler, then repaint. If a large area is affected, strip down to the plaster layer and make sure the wall is clean and dry (*see page 68*).

Finger marks Most modern paints are easily cleaned by washing with a proprietary wall cleaner liquid, but test an inconspicuous area first to check that the surface is stable.

Radiator marks Washing with a wall cleaner may help this problem, but the best cure is to fit a shelf above the radiator.

Dealing with damp walls

Peeling wallcoverings, brown water stains, and a white powdery deposit, called efflorescence, on plaster are all signs of a damp wall. First check that the dampness is not coming from leaking water pipes, waste pipes, downpipes or gutters. If the trouble is worse on a cold, dry day when the windows run with water, condensation is the probable cause of the problem. Cure this by improving ventilation, heating levels, and wall insulation (see Condensation, page 69).

If the trouble is worse in wet weather, there is a structural fault. Seek the advice of a damp-proofing contractor if the dampness is near to ground level or on a chimney breast. If the dampness is in isolated patches higher on the wall, suspect porous brickwork or some other fault such as bad pointing or cracks in an outside wall. Porous brickwork can be cured by painting the bricks with a clear silicone water-repellent liquid. For other repairs, see Exterior walls, page 54.

Preventing damp Although they do not cure the dampness, there are several interior damp-proofing liquids for walls and ceilings. These can be painted on to the wet or dry surface and will dry to form a seal which can be painted or wallpapered over. If efflorescence is on the wall it is best to damp-proof it with a waterproof laminate which is fixed to the wall using a special adhesive such as BP Aquaseal Damp Barrier Kit.

Repairing holes and channels in walls

Filling holes Chip away plaster until only firm plaster surrounds the hole. If there is a solid surface, such as bricks, under the plaster coat proceed as follows. (If there is a cavity under the plaster, see Ceilings page 16.) Brush away dust and fill the hole with a cellulose filler. Leave the filler slightly proud of the surface and when dry rub it down level using an abrasive block.

It is more economical to fill larger holes with a plaster filler. In this case dampen the area with water then apply the filler in layers until the surface is built up. If a large patch is being repaired it is a good idea to scrape the edge of a long straight board across the wet plaster to leave it flat. When this plaster has almost set, spray it with water, then rub it over with a steel float to leave a smooth finish.

Filling large holes Fill deep holes in brick or blockwork with cement mortar and pieces of brick. The plaster surface can then be built up as described above, although if a very large area is involved it is best to buy a ready-mixed browning plaster for the thick undercoat layer, and a ready-mixed finish plaster for the surface layer, which should be about 2 to 3mm (⅛in) thick.

Filling electric cable channels Electric cables can be buried in walls and plastered over. They can be held in place prior to plastering with moulded plastic steel pin cable clips which can be driven into the brickwork. Alternatively, use small scraps of wood as wedges to hold the cables in the channels, or use dabs of plaster. Dampen the channel and fill as described for large holes.

Fitting wall plugs If screws come loose from a plaster wall the holes will need refilling to provide extra support. You may also need longer screws which should penetrate the brickwork. To insert a plug, fill the hole with Polyfilla. If you need to drill a bigger hole, let the Polyfilla set. Drill hole with a masonry bit, and push in the new piece of wall plug.

Windows

Troubles with windows and doors are very similar; draughts, sticking, water penetration, broken glass and warping. Different problems affect metal windows and doors.

Most of these problems are straightforward to cure, but because of weather, the time has to be chosen carefully.

With metal windows, rust can cause broken glass, and the treatment is always expensive. All the glass must be replaced after preparing the frame and protecting it against further corrosion, or a new window may be necessary.

When replacing windows, two points should be borne in mind. Double glazed metal windows have about the same rate of heat loss as single glazed timber windows, because the metal has an extremely high U-value. Consider, too, the overall appearance of the house; will modern style metal windows, in bright aluminium, suit your period style cottage?

Cracked and broken glass

Repairing cracked glass Simple cracks in ordinary window glass are easy to repair with a special sealer such as 3M Glass Crack sealer. The sealer is a two-part resin which makes the crack virtually invisible and can save a great deal of work in replacing a pane and the cost of new glass.

It does not matter if the crack goes right across the pane, but if one piece of glass is slightly proud of the other, or if dirt has entered the crack, the repair will be visible, although the crack should be sealed. Do not use the sealer on a severe crack with more than one split.

On glass thicker than normal, that is, 4mm or more thick, the result may not be an invisible mend because the crack may not completely fill with resin.

The pane should be cleaned with a *dry* tissue, not with water or cleaning fluids. If the window has been exposed to rain, wait two days for it to dry thoroughly.

The sealer is supplied in a two-part sachet. Rolling one end of the sachet breaks the centre seal and forces the two liquids together. Work the sachet up and down with your fingers to mix the liquids thoroughly.

Pour the liquid into the small plastic applicator dish supplied in the kit. The applicator is used to run a thin line of resin along the crack on one side of the glass only. After 48 hours, excess resin is removed with a razor blade and the pane cleaned with window cleaning fluid. On textured glass the resin is removed with a scouring pad. The repair will continue to develop its optimum strength and

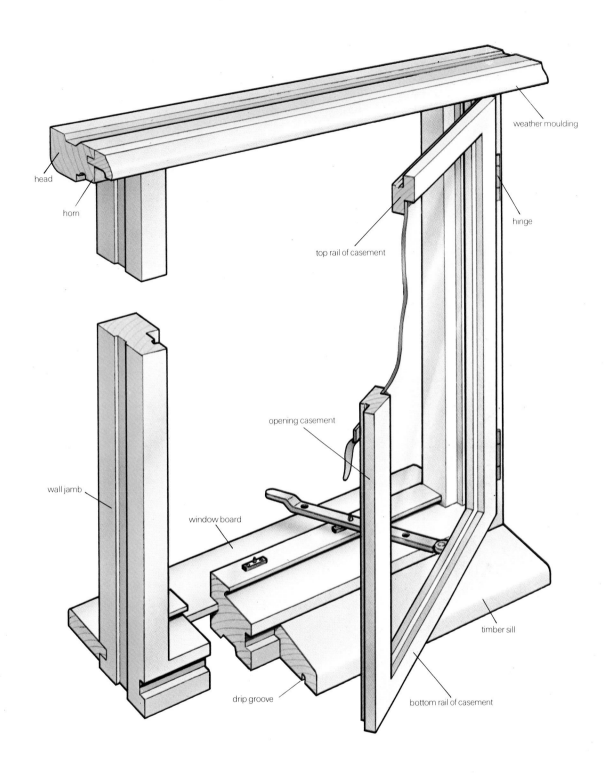

head

horn

weather moulding

top rail of casement

hinge

opening casement

wall jamb

window board

timber sill

drip groove

bottom rail of casement

appearance over the following two weeks.
Replacing broken glass For an emergency repair until new glass can be obtained, see page 90.

Removing the old glass can be dangerous so wear thick leather gloves and protect the eyes with plastic safety spectacles or goggles. Keep children and pets well away from the area until all the glass has been cleared up, wrapped in several layers of newspaper and put in the dustbin.

First remove those pieces of glass which are likely to drop out. The pane will probably be held with putty which will have hardened, but it may be held with narrow strips of wood called beadings.

In the latter case remove the beadings by carefully prising them away from the frame

ABOVE: *Cutaway diagram showing the structure of a basic casement window and details of its various components.*

When replacing broken glass wear thick leather gloves and safety spectacles.
1. Removing beadings from the frame with a chisel.
2. Chipping away old putty from putty-fixed glass with a hammer and chisel.
3. Removing glazing sprigs with pincers.

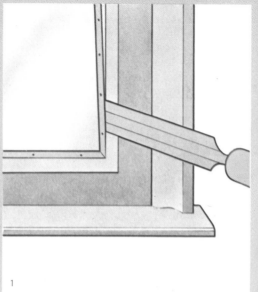

1

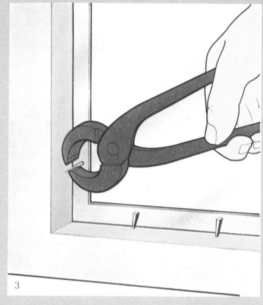

3

2

using an old chisel (*see diagram 1*). Work from the middle of the beading and there will be little risk of damaging the mitred ends which form neat corners. The beadings will be held with panel pins which must be removed with pincers if they remain in the frame.

Old putty can be removed with a hacking knife or old chisel and hammer (*see diagram 2*). The putty will probably come away in sections, but be careful not to damage the frame. If the putty is very hard it may be very difficult to remove. A blowtorch with a fine point flame should soften the putty, but be careful not to play the flame on the glass in case it splinters.

Small headless tacks called glazing sprigs will be found embedded in parts of the putty, and these must be removed with pincers (*see diagram 3*). In the case of metal frame windows the glass will be held with metal clips embedded in the putty and these should be saved for re-use.

With the putty or glazing beads removed, the remaining pieces of glass can be taken out of the frame. This is the dangerous part; sticking a piece of brown paper over the pane can help to reduce splintering. It will probably be necessary to tap the glass with the end of a hammer handle to free it. Take it out from the top of the frame first, then the sides, and finally from the bottom of the frame.

Use an old chisel to clean out the remaining putty in the window rebate. If necessary smooth the wood with glasspaper, brush out dust and apply a generous coat of primer which is left to dry. If the glass is held by wood beadings, these should also be primed.

In the case of metal window frames, considerable corrosion may be found if the frame has not been galvanised; in fact, the corrosion may have been responsible for the broken glass. Carefully chip away all the rust, rub down with medium coarse abrasive paper and treat the frame with a rust-killing liquid or primer. When this has dried, apply a zinc-based metal primer.

When measuring up for the new sheet of glass, deduct 6mm (¼in) from the width and height measurements to give a 3mm (⅛in) gap all round the frame. Check that the diagonal measurements between the corners of the frame are equal, indicating that the frame is square. If it is out of true it will be necessary to make a cardboard or paper template, or pattern for the replacement piece of glass. A template will be required for curved windows.

Check the new glass for fit in the frame and prepare the putty for use by kneading it in the hands. Special putty is required for metal window frames. Roll the putty in a ball and apply it all around the rebate of the frame by feeding it between the first finger and thumb. Make sure it is well pressed into the frame.

Settle the glass into position by pressing it around the edges only, never in the middle.

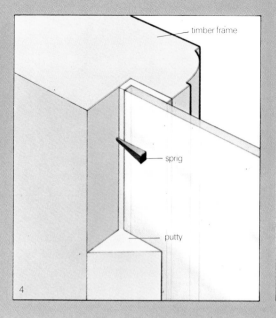

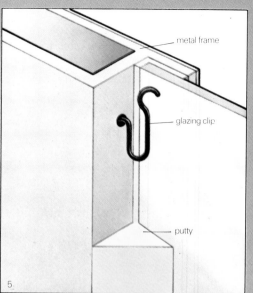

Make sure that obscured or patterned glass is fitted with the smooth side facing the outside.

The glass should rest in the rebate of the frame on a bed of putty 2mm to 3mm (¹/₁₆in to ⅛in) thick. Hold it in place with glazing sprigs in the case of a wood frame (*see diagram 4*), or wire clips if the frame is metal (*see diagram 5*).

Glazing sprigs, which are also called cut brads, resemble wedges of metal with sharp points. They should be about 15mm (½in) long and are inserted about 75mm (3in) from each corner of the frame and at about 300mm (12in) intervals elsewhere. They must be tight against the glass and are fitted by tapping home with the edge of a chisel which is slid across the glass.

Collect up the putty which exudes from the back of the glass, then place another bead of putty around the outer edge of the frame. With a putty knife, smooth this putty to a neatly angled fillet. If the result is not perfect, add more putty and try again. Practice makes perfect!

Leave the putty for about a fortnight to harden slightly before painting.

If the glass is held by wood beadings, bed the glass on putty as described above, but do not insert glazing sprigs. When the glass is settled, apply a thin final layer of putty on the front of the frame and press the beading into this, against the glass so it is held secure. Fix the beading in place with panel pins.

Replacing a broken sash cord

Remove the inside beads on either side of the window. Use a chisel and prise the beads out from the middle of the window to keep the mitre joints intact at the top and bottom.

Lift the lower sash into the room, cut the sash cords if these are still intact (replace all cords even if only one is broken) and with some string secured to the upper end, release each cord carefully so the balance weight drops to the bottom of its box. The string will be used to pull the new cords into place.

Prise the parting beads out of their grooves. These are the beads which separate the sashes. This will allow the top sash to be lifted into the room when the cords have been cut.

Use pincers and a screwdriver to prise out the nails holding the cords to the sides of the sashes. The sides of the frame are box sections in which the counterbalance weights hang. To give access to the weights, the pocket covers on each side of the frame must first be removed. The weights can be lifted through the pocket openings leaving the strings temporarily in place ready to pull the new cords through.

To rethread a pulley where a cord has broken, a nail (called a mouse) is tied to a length of string and the nail is fed over the pulley and pulled out through the pocket at the bottom of the frame. Use terylene cords for the replacements as these are far superior to the old fashioned cords.

Tie the cord to the string so it can be pulled

RIGHT: *Cutaway diagram showing the structure of a typical timber window frame with a sash mechanism.*

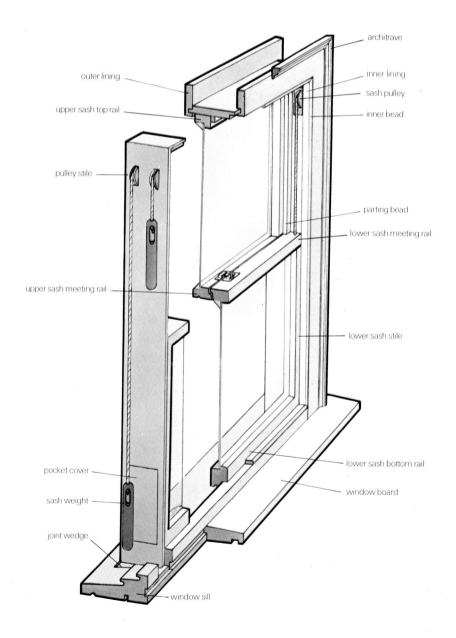

outer lining

upper sash top rail

pulley stile

upper sash meeting rail

pocket cover

sash weight

joint wedge

window sill

architrave

inner lining

sash pulley

inner bead

parting bead

lower sash meeting rail

lower sash stile

lower sash bottom rail

window board

over the pulley and out through the pocket (*see diagram 6*). Thread the cord through the hole in the balance weight and knot it so it is held securely. Hold the cut end of the cord above a lighted match for a few seconds to melt the fibres and prevent the end from fraying. Do this to all cut ends.

Fix the upper (outer) sash first. Measure the distance from the mid-point of the pulley to the top of the frame and mark this distance down on the side of the sash (*see diagram 7*). The upper sash cord securing nail must not be higher than this point or the window will not close properly.

Rest the sash on the window ledge, pull down each cord so the weight is at the top of its box and secure the cord to the side of the sash using several 25mm (1in) galvanised clout nails (*see diagram 8*). Put the sash in place and check that it operates correctly without the weights hitting the top or bottom of the boxes.

Fit the weights and cords for the lower sash, then replace the pocket covers and parting beads. Fit the lower sash in the same manner as the upper sash and check that the sash operates correctly. Finish the job by refitting the beads.

Repairing badly fitting windows

Easing a sticking window If the trouble is caused by a build-up of paint, get back to bare wood using paint stripper or a blowlamp. Check that there is adequate clearance (about 1.5mm/^{1}/$_{16}$in) between the window and the frame before repainting.

If damp has caused the wood to swell, strip off the paint, and dry the wood by gently playing a blowlamp flame over it. When dry, rub down with glasspaper or use a plane to give about 1.5mm (^{1}/$_{16}$in) clearance all round. Check putty and repaint the window to ensure that the wood is sealed against damp.

If the window is binding hard up against the hinge side, put a piece of thin cardboard under the hinge flap.

If the trouble is due to loose or broken joints in the frame, a simple cure is to screw flat steel L-shaped corner plates over the joints. Shut the window and drive small wedges between the window and the frame to close the joints before fitting the corner plates.

The repair will look neater if the plates are fitted flush with the surface of the window by recessing the wood with a chisel, rather as hinge flaps are fitted. Afterwards smooth the surface with a filler to give an invisible repair after painting.

Another way of tackling loose joints is to remove the window and close the joints using a web clamp, sash cramp or Spanish windlass, made by looping cord round the frame and twisting a stick around in the loop to tighten it. Drill into the joints and glue hardwood dowels in the drill holes to repair the frame.

Curing a draughty window Self-adhesive foam draught excluder strip is the easiest to fit. It should be fitted in the frame rebate so the window closes on to the strip and does not rub against it. Make sure the rebate is clean and dry. If paint is flaking, remove it and repaint before applying the excluder strip. The strip is suitable for both wood and metal windows.

A sprung metal or hard plastic draught excluder strip is more expensive than foam strip, but it is longer lasting. It can be used on surfaces which slide together, so it is useful for draughtproofing sliding sash windows. It can be used only on timber windows. For metal windows proprietary snap-on metal sealing strips are available.

The spring type of draught excluder is nailed in place with tacks supplied. It is fitted to the reveal (side) edge of the window frame with the nailed side of the strip facing the side the window opens. When used to draughtproof sash windows, the strip is fitted to the side beads, and to the meeting rail of the top sash with the nails along the top edge.

Some double glazing systems will help to eliminate draughts, but will not be fully effective unless the major sources of the draughts are cured.

Repairs to window blinds

Repairing a Venetian blind If the mechanism does not work properly, the trouble is probably caused by dirt or rust. Undo the clips or brackets so the head rail can be removed and the mechanism cleaned. Use a brush to remove dust and fluff. Usually the mechanism requires no lubrication, but if it has ceased to operate it is worth trying a spray-on aerosol lubricant before buying a new mechanism.

The cord stop mechanism works by gravity and often gives trouble. Make sure it is clean and free, and that the cords are correctly seated in their grooves.

Fraying cords should be replaced before they break. Make sure the new cord is the correct size. Note how the old cord is threaded and fit the new cord in the same way.

Repairing a roller blind If the blind becomes slack in use, or does not stay in position correctly, the ratchet may not be properly tensioned. Pull the blind down about half way, lift it off the brackets, then roll it up to the top. Try the tension and make further adjustments as necessary.

The ratchet mechanism should not be oiled. If the mechanism fails to work properly, it may be necessary to buy a new wooden roller to which the blind fabric may be stapled. Spraying the faulty mechanism with an aerosol lubricant may help. The counter-balance weights on the ratchet mechanism will work more positively if each weight is loaded with a blob of solder.

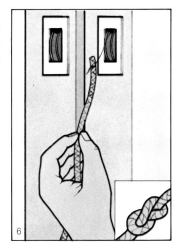

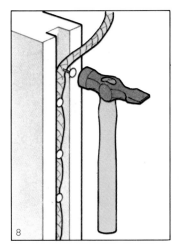

Replacing a damaged or broken sash cord.
6. *Pulling the new sash cord through the pulley opening.*
7. *Marking the mid-point of the pulley on the top sash.*
8. *Nailing the new cord in position on the bottom sash.*

Doors

Repairing badly fitting doors

Easing a sticking door The striking plate of the latch is often too far out from the door stop rebate of the frame. Close the door and clearly mark the position of the door face in relation to the frame.

Turn the latch and press the door into the frame. The distance that the door moves is the distance that the striking plate must be moved towards the rebate. Mark this line on the frame.

Remove the striking plate and chisel out the recess up to the pencil mark. Refix the striking plate, chisel out the recesses for the latch and dead bolt and test the door for fit.

Sealing a draughty door There are various types of draught excluders, such as buffer strip, brush, rubber flap and spring-assisted types, for fitting to the bottom of the door. (See page 29, Curing a draughty window, for the techniques involved.)

There are several ways to correct ill-fitting draughty doors. If a door is tight on the hinge side with a gap on the lock side (*see diagram 1*), put thin cardboard under the hinge flaps until the fault is corrected.

BELOW: *Cutaway diagram showing the structure of a typical door and frame, with details of its component parts.*

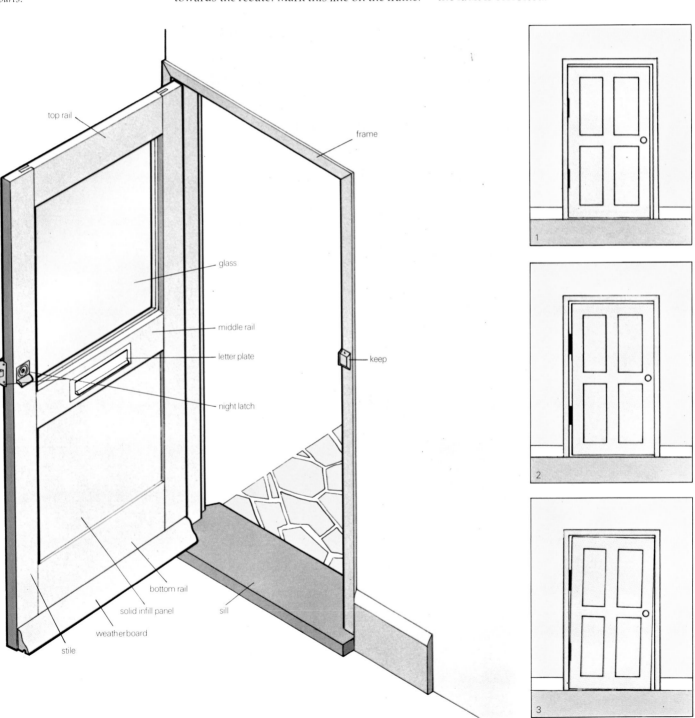

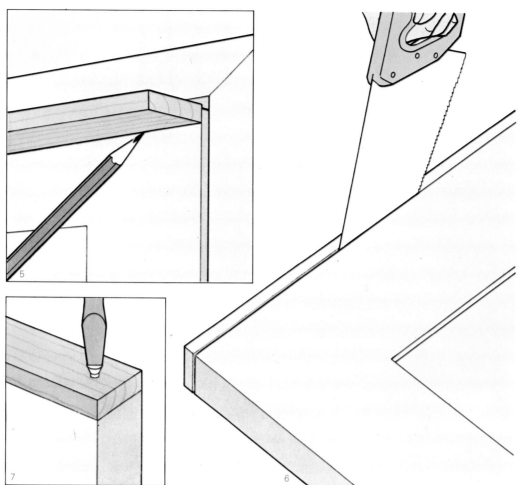

If a door is tight on the lock side with a gap on the hinge side (*see diagram 2*), remove the hinges and use a chisel to increase the depth of the recesses. If possible, avoid making alterations to the lock side.

If the hinge pins are worn or the hinges loose, causing the door to drop (*see diagram 3*), fit new hinges or tighten the hinge securing screws. If the screw holes are enlarged, glue wood dowels into them, redrill pilot holes, and refix the screws.

Where the door and frame are badly distorted (*see diagram 4*), the gaps can be closed with filler strips fitted to the door. These strips should be fractionally wider than the thickness of the door, and thick enough to close the gap (allowing about 3mm (⅛in) clearance) at the widest point.

With the door closed, hold a strip against the frame and mark its position on the door (*see diagram 5*). Remove the door and take off hinges. Plane or saw the edge of the door to the pencil marks (*see diagram 6*).

The strip is glued to the edges of the door with a pva adhesive and fixed with countersunk head wood screws (*see diagram 7*). Plane the edges of the strip smooth with the face of the door. Cut new recesses for the hinge flaps, if a filler strip was fitted to the hinge side, and refix the hinges using longer screws to compensate for the packing strip.

Refitting a warped door It may be possible to compensate for a warped door by moving one or more of the hinges. If the door stop beading of the frame can be removed the warp can be accommodated by renailing the beading against the door with the door closed.

A warp in a garage door can often be corrected by fitting a wire brace across the door to pull the door back into line. Make the brace from plaited fence straining wire. Anchor the brace at each end by looping the wire through steel plates screwed to the door. In the middle of the brace fit an adjustable screwed shackle so that tension on the wire can be gradually increased as the warp is corrected. Push a block of wood between the brace and the door to create a cantilever which will increase the pressure on the warp.

Stopping water from coming under a door Screw a weatherboard to the bottom of the door. This is a shaped piece of hardwood or metal with a drip groove along its bottom edge to throw water away from the bottom of the door.

Open the door and cut the weatherboard to fit the width of the door. Hold the weatherboard against the door frame stops and mark its outline on the frame. Carefully chisel out this shape so that when the weatherboard is screwed to the door, it will close properly. Prime the underside and the back of the weatherboard and glue and screw it in place. It will be necessary to round the ends of the weatherboard slightly so the door will open and close easily.

Fitting new handles and locks

Fitting a new door handle (*see diagrams 8 and 9*) Remove the screw holding the old handle on the shaft, which will allow the other handle and operating bar to be removed. Undo the screws holding the escutcheon or rosette plates and remove them. Fill any screw holes which will show after the new handles have been fitted.

Fit the operating bar in the new handle to position the handle correctly in relation to the lock, then screw in place. It will probably be a lever handle complete with lever plate. Fix the second handle over the operating bar. It may be necessary to cut a small piece off the operating bar so that the handle will meet the door.

Replacing a mortise lock (*see diagram 9*) Release the screws holding the handles and remove them together with the operating bar. Remove the key. Undo the screws holding the face plate to the edge of the door and lever the lock out of place using a screwdriver in the keyhole as a lever.

It may be possible to repair the old lock. Remove the side plate and check the springs and lubricate the mechanism. If repair is impossible, buy a new lock of the same size as the old one with handle and key positions in identical places.

Slide the new lock into place; it may be necessary to chisel out the opening. Refit the face plate screws, handles and escutcheons. It may be necessary to replace the striker plate with a new one.

Replacing a rim lock or night latch (*see diagram 10*) On the inside of the door remove the screws holding the latch case and check that this part is working properly; there may be no need to replace it. Two screws through a metal plate hold the cylinder in place. The cylinder will push out through the front of the door.

For security, replace with a key-operated deadlocking latch. With this type the lock can be secured with a turn of the key and even if the glass beside the latch is broken, the latch handle cannot be turned.

Fitting is a reversal of the dismantling procedure, but if the lock is not the same model as the type removed, follow the manufacturer's fitting instructions.

Repairs to door frames

Repairing a rotted door frame The rot is usually at the base of the frame and this part can be repaired without replacing the entire frame. Cut straight into a sound part of the frame with a sloping cut to minimise rain penetration. Lever away the rotted part. Make a second cut slightly above the first but only half way through the frame. Chisel away the wood between the cuts to form a step (*see diagram 11*). Carefully measure up and cut a new piece to fit the opening. Treat the new wood and cut surfaces with clear or green grade timber preservative and allow to dry. Glue the new section in place using screws and waterpoof glue where it joins the old timber, and screws and wallplugs, or masonry nails, where it joins the wall. If the frame incorporates a door stop rebate, a batten to match up with the existing door stop can be nailed on to the new section after fitting.

Fixing a loose frame Scrape out dirt and loose mortar from between the frame and the wall. Get a piece of wood slightly wider than the door width and, with one end wedged at the base of the frame, press down on the other end to force the frame back to the wall. Using a long masonry

8. *How to dismantle a non-locking door latch, usually fitted on internal doors.*

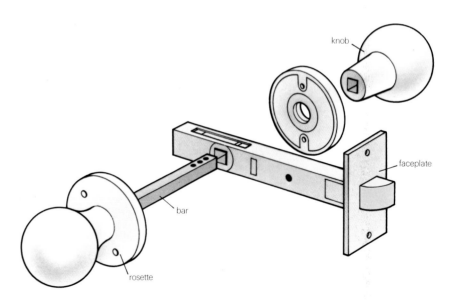

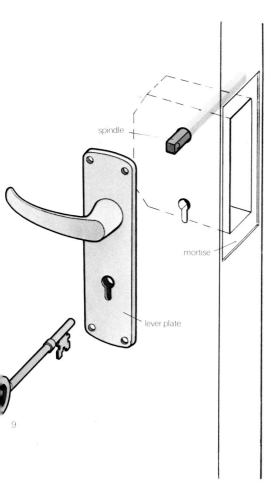

spindle

mortise

lever plate

9

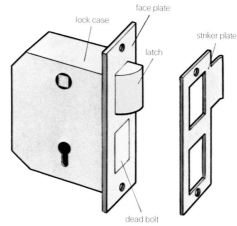

lock case

face plate

latch

striker plate

dead bolt

9. *A mortise door latch and lock in a single unit, used for both internal and external doors.*
10. *A cylinder or rim lock has a night latch, and is commonly fitted to an entrance door.*
11. *Replacing a piece of door frame which has been eroded by rot. The new piece is screwed into place.*

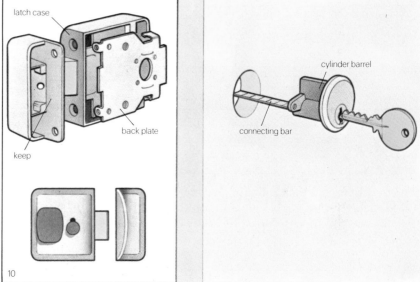

latch case

back plate

keep

cylinder barrel

connecting bar

10

drill bit, drill through the frame and about 60mm (2½in) into the wall. Push a wallplug through the hole in the frame and about 50mm (2in) into the wall. It may be necessary to countersink the hole to allow the screw head and washer to go neatly below the surface of the frame. Finally, press filler over the screwhead to leave a smooth surface.

Curing gaps between door and window frames and walls Because of the natural movement of wood, these gaps need a flexible filler. Rake out the old mortar and remove dust with a brush.

The filler, a non-hardening flexible mastic, is injected into the gap to leave a neat bead of mastic. These mastics are available in white, brown or grey and are supplied in tubes with plastic nozzles which can be trimmed to give the desired thickness of mastic. The pack may have a special screw-down applicator or be designed for use with a metal mastic applicator gun. Although the mastic never hardens, it does form a thin skin which can easily be painted over if desired.

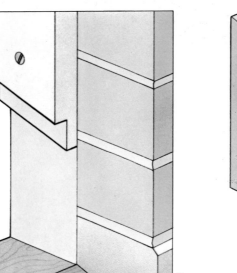

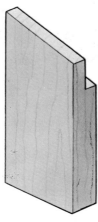

11

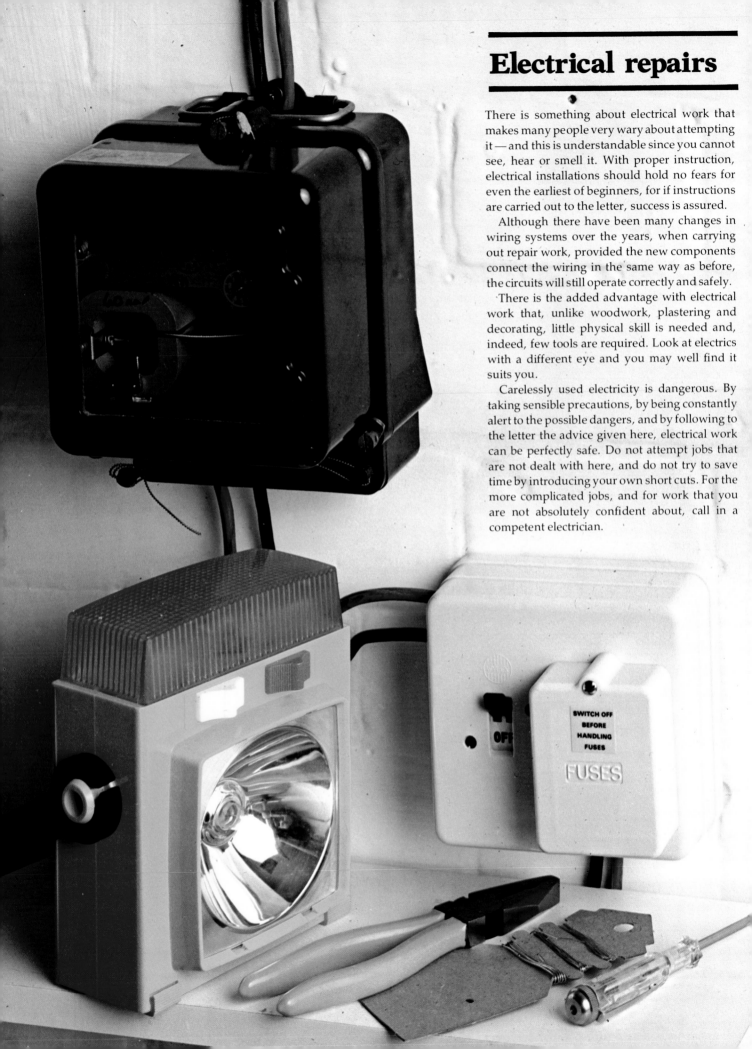

Electrical repairs

There is something about electrical work that makes many people very wary about attempting it — and this is understandable since you cannot see, hear or smell it. With proper instruction, electrical installations should hold no fears for even the earliest of beginners, for if instructions are carried out to the letter, success is assured.

Although there have been many changes in wiring systems over the years, when carrying out repair work, provided the new components connect the wiring in the same way as before, the circuits will still operate correctly and safely.

There is the added advantage with electrical work that, unlike woodwork, plastering and decorating, little physical skill is needed and, indeed, few tools are required. Look at electrics with a different eye and you may well find it suits you.

Carelessly used electricity is dangerous. By taking sensible precautions, by being constantly alert to the possible dangers, and by following to the letter the advice given here, electrical work can be perfectly safe. Do not attempt jobs that are not dealt with here, and do not try to save time by introducing your own short cuts. For the more complicated jobs, and for work that you are not absolutely confident about, call in a competent electrician.

SWITCH OFF
BEFORE
HANDLING
FUSES

FUSES

OFF

Electrical safety rules

Follow these rules before tackling any electrical repairs or carrying out inspection work.

Always disconnect the equipment from the power supply.

To work on permanently wired equipment, such as switches and socket outlets, turn off the electricity supply at the mains switch on the consumer unit (the main fuse box) and remove the fuse of the appropriate circuit at the consumer unit (main fuse box).

To work on an appliance, remove the plug from the socket outlet before inspecting or working on the equipment. Do not merely switch off at the socket outlet as this does not ensure isolation.

If the appliance does not have a removable plug, like an extractor fan, treat it as permanently wired equipment.

Fault finder

If one appliance fails, suspect a blown fuse in its plug; try another appliance or a table lamp in the same socket outlet.

If the socket outlet appears to be dead, suspect a blown fuse in the consumer unit (main fuse box). If a fuse is at fault it is likely that a number of socket outlets on the same circuit will be out of action.

If one light fails, suspect a faulty bulb. If a number of lights fail, suspect a blown fuse in the consumer unit.

If every light and electrical appliance in the house fails, first check that there is not a general power cut affecting the neighbourhood then call in the electricity board to check their main sealed fuse which protects the supply meter and the entire household electrical system.

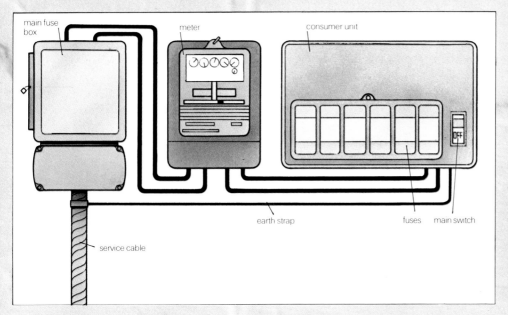

main fuse box

meter

consumer unit

earth strap

fuses   main switch

service cable

ABOVE: *Always remove the plug from the socket when doing an electrical repair.*

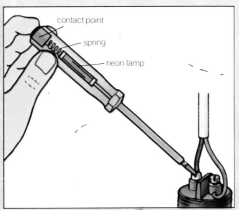

contact point

spring

neon lamp

ABOVE: *Checking terminals with a mains tester screwdriver, to ensure supply is turned off.*

Safety is of primary importance when handling electricity. If you are repairing permanently wired equipment, switch off at the mains switch in the consumer unit **(Above)**. OPPOSITE: *Very few tools are needed for electrical repairs. From left to right: a sturdy lamp, pliers, fuse wire and mains tester screwdriver.*

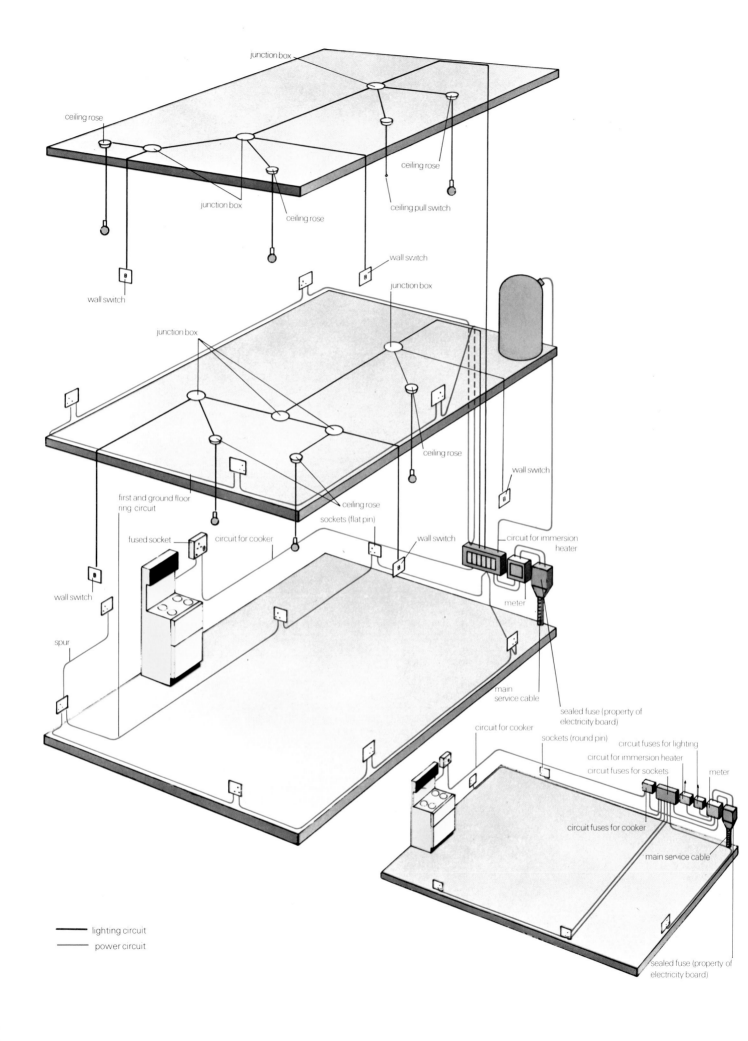

junction box

ceiling rose

junction box

ceiling rose

ceiling rose

ceiling pull switch

wall switch

wall switch

junction box

junction box

junction box

ceiling rose

wall switch

first and ground floor
ring circuit

ceiling rose

sockets (flat pin)

wall switch

circuit for immersion
heater

fused socket

circuit for cooker

wall switch

meter

wall switch

spur

main
service cable

sealed fuse (property of
electricity board)

circuit for cooker

sockets (round pin)

circuit fuses for lighting

circuit for immersion heater

circuit fuses for sockets

meter

circuit fuses for cooker

main service cable

sealed fuse (property of
electricity board)

—— lighting circuit

—— power circuit

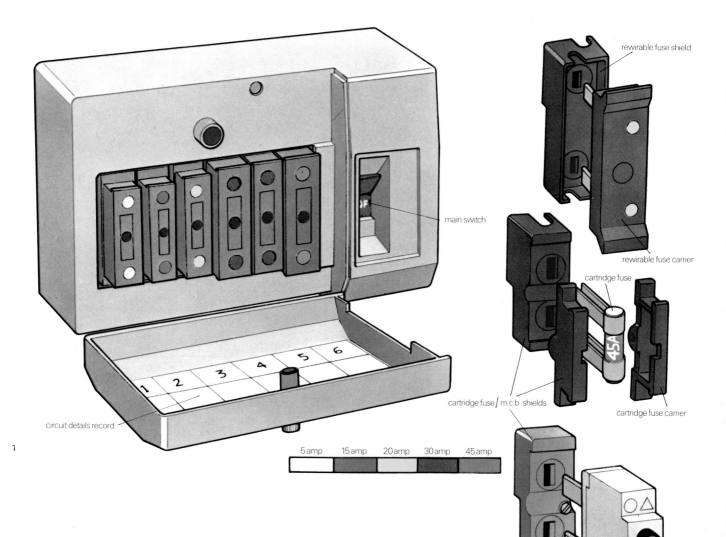

rewirable fuse shield

main switch

rewirable fuse carrier

cartridge fuse

cartridge fuse / m.c.b. shields

cartridge fuse carrier

circuit details record

1

5 amp   15 amp   20 amp   30 amp   45 amp

miniature circuit breaker

Fuses and contact breakers

Repairing or replacing fuses in a consumer unit When a number of lights or socket outlets fail to work, the fault is usually a blown fuse in the consumer unit or main fuse box, which is located close to the electricity board's supply meter.

Turn off at the main switch (remember NEVER work on live equipment) and remove the cover to gain access to the fuse carriers (*see diagram 1*). The cover should have labels inside listing each fuse carrier with the circuit it controls: with this information and knowing which circuit is out of operation, you should be able to tell immediately which fuse has blown.

If the fuse box cover does not carry details of each circuit you must remove each carrier in turn to find the blown fuse. Probably the carrier will be the rewireable type. In this case look for the carrier which has broken or melted fuse wire. The carrier may look slightly scorched, but sometimes a broken fuse wire is not immediately obvious and it will be necessary to tug at each end of the fuse wire with an electrical screwdriver to find out if the wire is firmly connected. If the carriers have cartridge fuses or miniature contact breakers, see below.

Cartridge fuse carriers This type has a cartridge fuse similar to the cartridge fuse fitted in a 13 amp plug. If the circuits are not marked you can check the fuse with a metal-cased torch, or a battery and bulb.

Switch off at the main switch and remove each fuse carrier in turn. Remove the cartridge fuse and connect it across the bottom of the battery and side of the torch casing, or between the battery terminal and bulb. If the fuse is sound the bulb will light (it may be only a glimmer).

Replace the faulty fuse for a new one — *never* attempt a repair. It is impossible to fit a fuse of the incorrect rating because the ratings, except for 15 and 20 amp, have different external dimensions.

5 amp fuses coloured white are for lighting circuits up to 1kW.

15 amp fuses coloured blue, and 20 amp fuses coloured yellow, are for immersion heater circuits of 3.6kW and 4.8kW respectively.

30 amp fuses coloured red are for ring circuits up to 7.2kW.

45 amp fuses coloured green are for cooker circuits up to 10.8kW.

Refit the fuse carrier and close the cover before turning on the main switch.

ABOVE LEFT: *Six-way consumer unit has rewireable fuse units – one 5 amp, one 15 amp, one 20 amp, two 30 amps and one 45 amp.*
ABOVE RIGHT: *The types of fuse units that can be fitted – rewireable, cartridge and miniature circuit breaker.*
LEFT *A typical wiring system.*

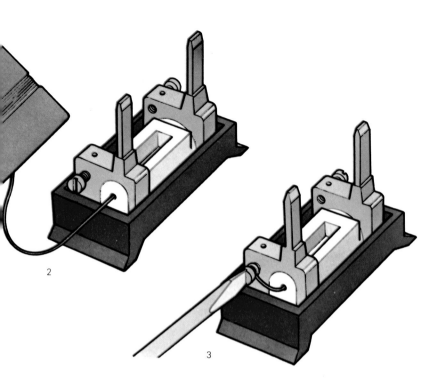

2

3

ABOVE: *Fitting a new fuse wire into a rewireable fuse carrier. Note that the wire goes around the fixing screw in a clockwise direction.*
RIGHT: *Old flex colour code* (**Left**) *and the new code* (**Right**).

Rewireable fuse carriers Note the route of the fuse wire in the carrier, or use another as a guide, then slacken the clamp screws and remove the pieces of old fuse wire.

Insert one strand of fuse wire of the correct rating, which is usually indicated on the fuse carrier (*see diagram 2*). If it is not marked, use 5 amp fuse wire for a lighting circuit, 15 amp wire for an immersion heater, and 30 amp wire for a ring main circuit. The fuse shields are often coloured, and the fuse carriers marked with the same coloured dots according to the rating of the fuse they should be carrying: white for 5 amp, blue for 15 amp and red for 30 amp.

Wind the end of the fuse wire clockwise around each clamp screw, or under the clamping plate, and tighten the screw (*see diagram 3*). Make sure that the wire is firmly attached, but not stretched.

Check that the fuse carrier contacts are smooth and clean before replacing the carrier and closing the cover. Switch off all the appliances or lights in the circuit supplied by the fuse before turning the main switch on. This will help you to find the fault which originally caused the fuse to blow.

The fuse is a guard against an overload, so it may have blown because there are too many appliances on the circuit, or because one of the appliances is faulty. If you suspect an appliance is faulty, take it to a qualified electrician to be checked and repaired. Sometimes a light bulb will blow the fuse as the filament breaks, and sometimes a fuse will blow because it is old.

Do not try to stop a fuse from blowing by fitting a higher rated one, or a double strand of fuse wire. If a fuse blows after being replaced and you cannot find the fault, call in an electrician.

Miniature contact breakers These are sometimes found in consumer units instead of fuses. They automatically switch off if a circuit is overloaded. To reset the circuit breaker press in the reset button.

Testing and replacing a plug fuse Square-pin 13 amp plugs are fitted with cartridge fuses to protect individual appliances. If an appliance fails, remove the plug from its socket outlet and undo the cover retaining screw which will be found on the underside of the plug. When the cover is removed the cartridge fuse will be seen fitted between metal clips, from which it can be levered. Occasionally one end of the fuse is fitted in a hole in the live pin and the other end is fitted into a clip attached to the live wire terminal. In this case the pin slides out of the plug body to allow the fuse to be removed.

Test the fuse with a metal-cased torch or battery and bulb as for cartridge fuse carriers.

Replace a blown fuse with one of the correct rating. For appliances up to 720 watts (table lamps, black and white televisions), use a 3 amp fuse, coloured red. Above 720 watts up to 3kW (kettles, heaters, washing machines), use a 13 amp fuse, coloured brown. Some appliances (such as colour televisions, and spin dryers) although rated at less than 720 watts require a 13 amp fuse because they take a high starting current.

Before replacing the plug cover make sure the wires of the flex are connected to the correct terminals — the colour codings are given below. Also check that the connections are neat and that the terminal screws are tight.

If the fuse was blown, rectify the cause of the problem or consult an electrician before plugging the appliance back in a socket. Likely faults are broken wires in the flex, badly kinked, frayed, worn or burnt flex.

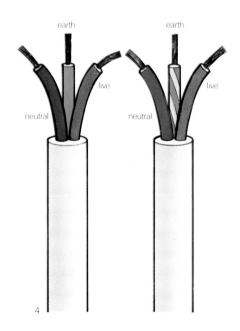

4

Rewiring a plug Never attempt repairs if the body of a plug becomes cracked or broken. Replace it immediately with a new plug.

Prepare the flex by removing about 50mm (2in) of the outer sheath. The best way to do this is to bend the flex double and cut through the outer sheath with a sharp knife, but take care not to cut into the insulation of the core wires inside the sheath.

New flex will be coloured blue (the neutral wire), brown (the live wire) and green and yellow stripes (the earth wire) (*see diagram 4*). Two-core flex, which is intended for use with double-insulated appliances marked clearly with a square within a square, is coloured blue and brown.

In the case of old flex the black wire is neutral, the red wire live, and the green wire is the earth wire.

A plug with the cover removed (*see diagram 5*) shows the largest pin (the earth) at the top of the plug and the flex outlet at the bottom, the neutral terminal (marked N) on the left-hand side and the live terminal (marked L) on the right-hand side.

Place the flex in position over the plug and cut the core wires so they reach about 12mm (½in) past the terminals to which they will be fitted. With wire strippers or a sharp knife, trim about 12mm (½in) of insulation from each core, being careful not to cut the wires, then twist the wires of each core neatly together.

Now place the flex in position in the plug, either under the screw-down clamp-type flex grip, or between the nylon arms of a V-shaped flex grip. If the plug has screw hole terminals (*see diagram 6*), double back the twisted wires and push them fully into the correct terminal holes. Tighten the pinch screws to anchor the wires firmly.

If the plug has clamp type terminals (*see diagram 7*), remove the nuts and curl the wires clockwise around the terminal posts, then tighten the clamp nuts.

Replacing a light flex and lampholder

Lampholders and light flex are subjected to a considerable amount of heat from a light bulb and they must be checked for damage from time to time.

Switch off the electricity supply at the main switch and remove the appropriate fuse to isolate the circuit: even with the wall switch off, there could still be live wires to the ceiling rose.

Look for cracking, hardening and signs of scorching on the light flex, and for cracked and broken plastic insulation around the lampholder. Use an insulated screwdriver to push the lampholder plungers up and down. There should be firm tension, but the plungers should slide freely.

To fit a new light flex, unscrew the ceiling rose cover and with the tip of the blade of a mains tester screwdriver touch each of the terminals in turn to double check that the circuits are completely dead.

Note how the wires are fitted, then loosen the terminal screws to release the two-core light flex. Cut the new flex to the length of the old, plus about 100mm (4in). Remove about 50mm (2in) of the outer protective sheath from each end taking care not to cut into the insulation of the wires inside.

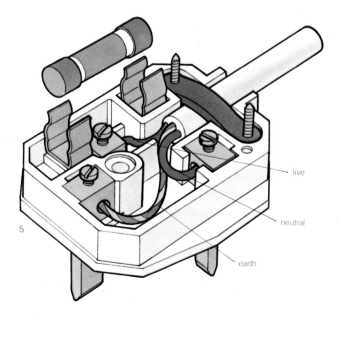

BELOW: *A fused 13 amp plug showing the fuse fitting and the flex anchor strip.*
LEFT: *Two kinds of plug terminal clamps and the methods of wiring them.*

live

neutral

earth

5

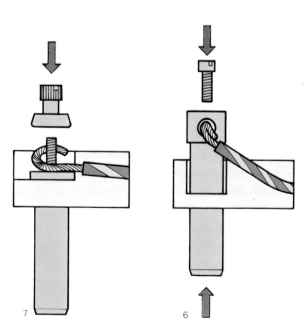

7   6

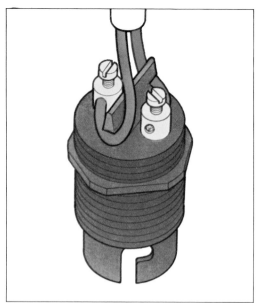

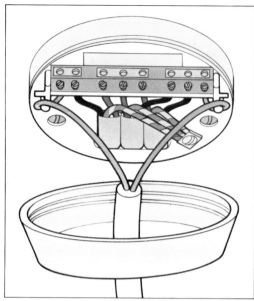

Position the wires in the lampholder (*see above*) and cut them 12mm (½in) longer than necessary to reach the terminals. Remove 12mm (½in) of insulation from the end of each wire, twist the conductor strands together, and then double them over on themselves.

Push each wire into a terminal hole and tighten the clamp screw. It does not matter to which terminal the live (brown) wire is connected. Before sliding the lampholder cover down the flex, make sure the wires are correctly positioned under the lugs which take the strain of the light fitting.

The next stage is to fit the flex to the ceiling rose. First slide the rose cover on to the flex. Hold the wires in position and once again cut them 12mm (½in) longer than necessary and prepare the ends as described above. Make the connections in the same way that the old flex was connected (the live, brown, wire of the flex goes to the live return from the switch).

Make sure the wires are correctly positioned under the straining lugs before the cover is replaced, and fit the shade and bulb.

Replacing a ceiling rose

Switch off at the mains and remove the appropriate fuse to isolate the circuit. Remove the ceiling rose cover and double check with a mains tester screwdriver that the terminals are completely dead.

The cover will unscrew in an anti-clockwise direction, but it may be very tight because of a build-up of paint affected by heat from the light. Often it helps to cut around the joint with a sharp knife where the cover and mounting block join.

It is most important to draw a diagram showing how all the wires are connected, before removing the old rose. You will need to know to which wires the flex is connected, and the connections of the cables which come through

from behind the rose. In the latter case it will probably be necessary to remove the screws holding the rose to the ceiling so the rose can be pulled down sufficiently for the cables to be identified.

When you are satisfied that you know how the connections are made, remove the old rose, and mounting block if one was fitted.

The new rose can be screwed direct to the ceiling because it will have an enclosed back. The fixing screws should go through the plaster and into solid timber. It may be necessary to fix a mounting board between the joists above the rose position. Before securing the fixing screws, break out the cable entry holes as required in the back of the new rose and bring the cables through.

The rose will probably have terminal blocks in a row but, using the wiring diagram you prepared, it should be possible to reconnect the wires in the original manner. The new rose will have provision for an earth connection but, unless your installation has an earth circuit, leave these terminals unconnected.

Before replacing the ceiling rose cover, make sure the flex wires are fitted under the straining lugs. Be sure to replace the flex and lampholder, as described above, if either of these is old.

Replacing a light switch

It is a straightforward job to replace a light switch, and it is no more difficult to change a conventional switch for a modern dimmer switch. The connections are the same and most dimmer switches are designed to fit into conventional plaster depth boxes.

Switch off at the mains and remove the appropriate fuse to isolate the circuit.

Plate switches are usually held with two screws at the front of the switch. Remove these screws and carefully ease the switch forward to avoid damaging the cables.

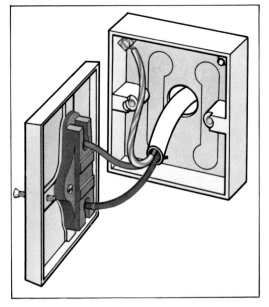

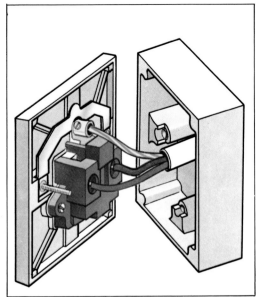

Use a mains tester screwdriver to check that all wires to the switch are dead. Before releasing the terminal screws note how the wires are connected. In the case of a two-way switch (where a light can be controlled from two points) there will be three wires, and possibly an earth wire connected to the box. Make a particular note of which wire is connected to the terminal marked common' because it must go to the 'common' terminal on the new switch.

When the new switch is fitted, make sure it is the right way up. If you have a two-way switch which will be used for one way only, connect the live wire to the terminal marked L2.

Position the new switch with the wires of the cables well away from the sides of the box so the wires will not be nipped when the switch securing screws are fitted.

If you are replacing an old fashioned surface mounted tumbler switch it will probably be best to mount the new switch in a plastic surface mounted box which can be screwed to the wall over the place where the old switch and wooden mounting block were fitted.

Replacing a damaged socket outlet

Switch off the electricity supply at the main switch and remove the appropriate fuse to isolate the circuit.

Remove the securing screws from the front of the plate and pull the socket outlet forward. Use a mains tester screwdriver to check that each terminal is dead. Remove the terminal screws.

If the new socket outlet is the same size as the old one, connect the red wire, or wires, to the terminal marked live (L), the black wire or wires to the terminal marked neutral (N), and the bare wires to earth (E). The earth wires should be covered with green and yellow striped earth sleeving which is slipped over the wires.

A 13 amp square pin socket outlet can be changed from the single to the double type provided it is on a main circuit, or is the only outlet on a branch or spur from a ring circuit. If the sockets are the round pin type they are obviously old, and so is the wiring, and a complete rewire is required by a professional electrician.

For a double socket, the existing ring circuit cables can be used, but a larger mounting box will be required. It is simple to fit a surface mounted box but the wall must be chiselled out for a flush mounting box.

Undo the fixing screws and remove the old box. Mark the plaster where the new box will go and with a masonry drill bit make a series of holes to box depth into the plaster to be removed. Clear out the hole with a small cold chisel. Remove the knockouts from the new box where the cables will enter it and fit rubber grommets into the holes to prevent chafing of the cables. Fit the box to the wall with 25mm (1in) gauge 8 woodscrews and wall plugs.

A double socket is connected in the same way as a single socket. If the new box has an earth terminal fixed to it, connect a length of single core earth wire about 120mm (5in) long between this terminal and the earth terminal on the socket outlet.

Repairing a door bell or chime

Switch off at the mains if the bell or chime operates through a transformer.

If a bell or chime fails to work, check for loose connections, a broken wire, or a faulty bell push. If it is battery operated, a new battery may be required.

If the bell or chime works intermittently, dirty connections are the likely cause. Clean well by rubbing a piece of cardboard between the contact spring and the screw. With both bells and chimes use a soft brush to clean dust from the mechanism and make sure the plunger moves freely.

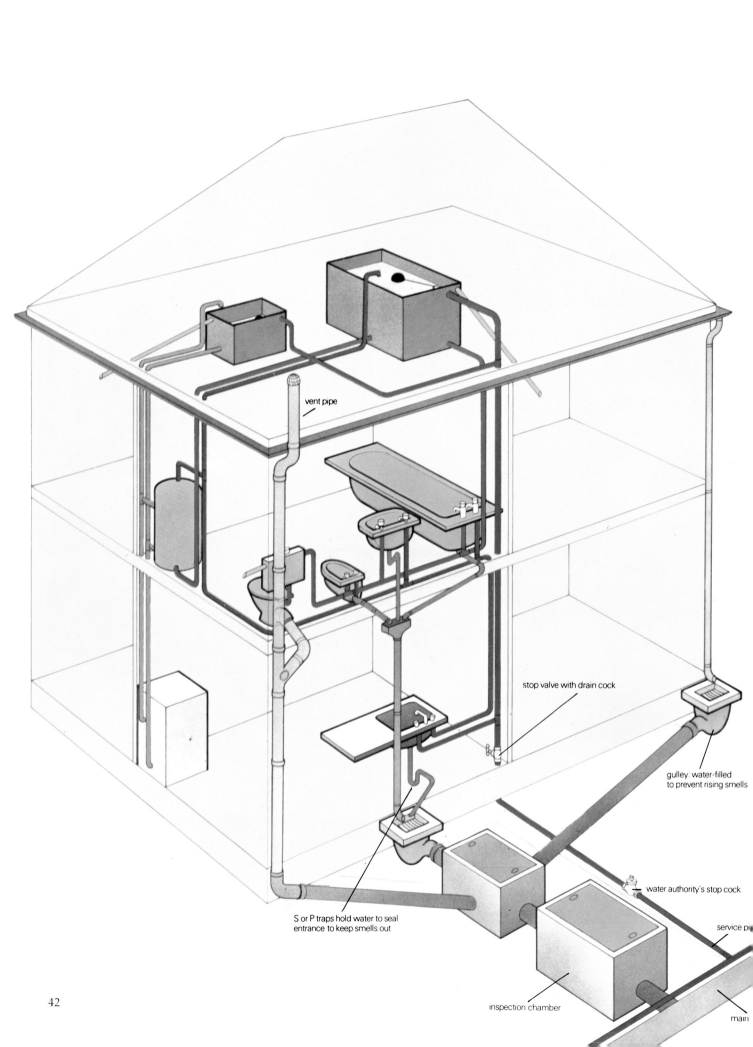

vent pipe

stop valve with drain cock

gulley: water-filled
to prevent rising smells

water authority's stop cock

service pi

S or P traps hold water to seal
entrance to keep smells out

inspection chamber

main

42

Plumbing

In the Good Old Days (?) plumbing was indeed a very skilled occupation with lots of lead pipes, wiped joints and mysterious goings-on with red lead and putty. Nowadays, things are so much different, with easy-to-make copper joints, push-on plastic connections for waste pipes and nary a piece of lead in sight. No need at all for the oft-quoted plumbers' nightmares!

Why is it that many fight shy of plumbing works? Is it that old mystique that puts them off? If so, get it out of sight, for pretty well any job in the modern home is well within most people's capability, from plumbing in a new shower to installing central heating.

Burst or split pipes

Burst or split pipes are quite easy to patch up. First, turn off the water supply. Then a piece of plastic pipe, such as garden hose, can be slipped over the damaged pipe. Position the hose over the break and secure it with hose clips at each end. Alternatively, wrap the pipe with a waterproof mastic bandage.

A more permanent repair of copper, lead, iron and plastic pipes can be made with glass fibre. Dry the pipe and clean the outside with a file. If possible, close the split by tapping the edges with a hammer.

Paint the outside of the pipe with clear resin, bind the pipe with glass fibre tape and stipple more resin into the tape. Clear resin and glass fibre tape are usually supplied in car bodywork repair kits. Sometimes a successful repair can be made with glass fibre paste built up all round the pipe after careful cleaning. The paste is the same as that used to fill dents in car bodywork. Make sure the glass fibre has set before turning on the water.

Splits in copper pipe can be permanently repaired by inserting a new piece of pipe. Use a hacksaw to cut out the affected section and use two straight compression connectors to join the new piece. The nuts on the connectors are tightened with spanners to make a watertight joint. If you take the damaged piece of pipe to a plumber's merchant you will be sure of getting new pipe and connectors of the right size.

If water freezes in a pipe, joints may be pushed apart. This is quite common with copper pipe joined with compression fittings. Slacken the nut on the fitting by turning it anti-clockwise, push the pipe back into the fitting as far as it will go, and tighten the nut securely by turning clockwise (*see diagram 1*).

Repairs to taps

Changing a tap washer A tap that continues to drip when turned off fully is in need of a new washer. The only items needed to change a washer are an adjustable wrench, pliers, suitable spanner and a new washer.

Sink and basin taps need 12.7mm (½in) washers; bath taps need 19mm (¾in) washers. The washer is attached to the jumper and is secured by a small nut. Often it is difficult to remove the small retaining nut, and it may be more convenient to fit a new jumper with washer attached.

With most types of tap it is necessary to turn off the water supply. The exception is a Supatap which can be rewashered without cutting off the water supply.

The cold tap over the kitchen sink is supplied direct from the rising main, and the main stopcock must be turned off. This stopcock is usually found in a readily accessible place, most often under the kitchen sink. Sometimes it is found outside the house in a purpose-made pit. Turn off the stopcock and run dry the cold tap over the sink.

All other taps in the house (both hot and cold)

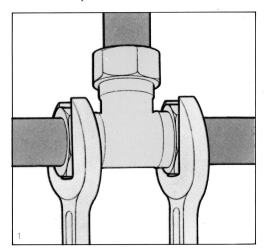

OPPOSITE: *The typical plumbing layout in an average house. The central heating pipework has not been included here.*
1. *Securing joints on compression fittings which have been pushed apart by freezing.*

mains supply	waste water
tank cold feed	overflow pipes
hot feed	boiler primary circuit

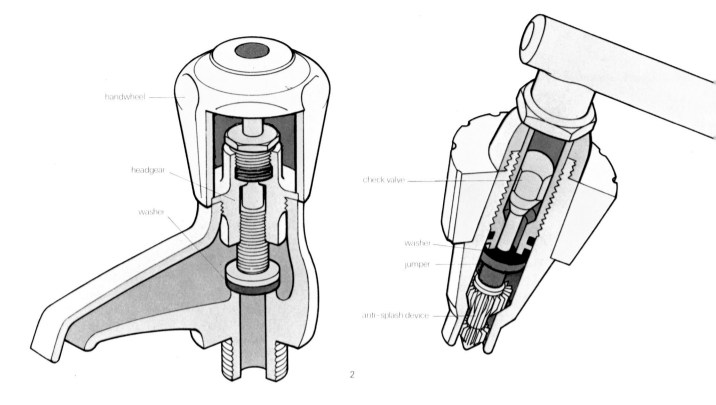

handwheel

headgear

washer

check valve

washer

jumper

anti–splash device

2

ABOVE: *Cutaway diagrams showing the component parts of a pillar tap* **(Left)** *and a Supatap* **(Right)**. *The inset diagram shows in detail how the washers are secured in both kinds of taps. These taps illustrate the two basic methods of fitting washers; there are several other kinds of taps, which vary in their external 'cladding'.*

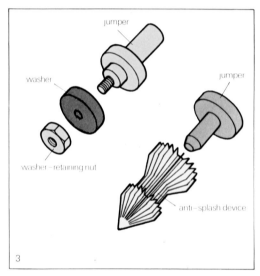

jumper

washer

jumper

washer–retaining nut

anti–splash device

3

are usually supplied from the cold water storage cistern. To stop water flowing into this cistern from the rising main supply pipe, raise the arm of the ball valve and keep it raised by tying it with a length of string from just behind the float and attaching the string to a convenient roof timber, or place a batten across the tank and tie the string to this. The tap to be rewashered can now be drained.

For a hot tap, tie up the ball valve, turn on the bathroom cold taps and allow them to run dry. The hot tap to be rewashered can then be allowed to run dry. Only a small amount of hot water will be lost, as the hot water storage cylinder will remain full.

An alternative is to turn off the stopcock feeding the hot water cylinder.

An older style tap will have its headgear

exposed. Use a suitable spanner or an adjustable wrench to unscrew the large hexagonal nut above the tap body and remove the headgear.

Some taps have an easy clean cover which may be removable by hand. If not, use a wrench with its jaws padded to prevent damage to the chromium plating of the cover. The large hexagonal nut will now be exposed and can be unscrewed. If you do not have a suitable spanner or wrench take off the tap handle by loosening the small retaining grub screw and tapping upwards until the handle is free.

Some modern acrylic taps have shrouded heads. The handle and headgear are all in one unit. To take off the head, use the tip of a small screwdriver to prise up the plastic hot or cold water indicator and remove the fixing screw beneath.

Another type of shrouded head tap is held in place by a rubber O-ring. The head is removed by opening it fully and then giving a final twist.

The tap body encloses the jumper and washer unit which should pull out easily (*see diagram 2*). Grip the jumper with a pair of pliers and unscrew the washer retaining nut. If this proves impossible even after applying a little penetrating oil, fit a new washer and jumper complete. If the nut can be removed, fit the new washer, replace the nut and refit the jumper, inside the headgear. Reassemble the tap and turn on the water supply.

Sometimes the jumper will turn freely but cannot be removed. This type is pegged into the headgear. It is far easier to remove the washer retaining nut to replace only the washer. The alternative is to break the pegging by inserting a screwdriver between the jumper plate and the base of the headgear and forcing the jumper out. Before fitting a new washer and jumper, the stem of the jumper will have to be burred to achieve a really close fit between the stem of the jumper and the headgear.

To replace the washer on a Supatap, (*see diagram 3*) simply release the sleeve nut above the handle, which should be held firmly. Holding the sleeve nut revolve the tap fully until it comes right off. A certain amount of water will flow out as the tap is unscrewed but will soon stop. Press the tap nozzle on a hard surface to push out the antisplash device which houses the jumper and washer. To release the jumper, use a screwdriver blade to prise it upwards carefully. The special washer and jumper for a Supatap is bought complete for refitting in the antisplash device. Reassemble the tap.

Repacking a tap gland If water leaks around the tap spindle when the tap is turned on, the gland packing inside the head needs to be adjusted or renewed. This is also necessary for a tap that turns on and off too easily. This freedom of movement is often accompanied by a banging noise in the pipe when the tap is turned off. The noise is called water hammer and will be cured when the gland packing fault has been remedied.

Sometimes the leakage can be repaired quite simply by removing the easy clean cover (see rewashering) and tightening the gland adjusting nut a little with a half turn in a clockwise direction. If this fails to stop the leak, the tap head or handle will have to be removed. Many tap handles can be tapped off after removing the retaining grub screw, although others will be more difficult.

Turn off the water supply to the tap and open it up. Raise the easy clean cover and insert two pieces of wood between the base of the cover and the top of the tap body and turn off the tap. The pressure of the cover will gradually ease the handle off and enable the easy clean cover to be removed.

Remove the adjusting nut and pick out all the old packing with a screwdriver or penknife. Repack the gland with some darning wool coated with petroleum jelly. Wind this around the spindle. When replacing the gland nut, tighten it until the handle turns comfortably and firmly. Replace the easy clean cover and handle.

Some modern taps have rubber O-ring seals instead of packing, and the worn out seal is replaced with a new one.

Repairs to tanks and cisterns

Ball-valve washer Water gushing from an overflow pipe indicates a leaking ball valve float, or the need for a new washer on the ball valve (*see diagram 4 and 5*) in the cold water storage tank in the roof space, or in the lavatory cistern.

Unscrew the ball from its arm, shake it and listen for water inside it. If you can hear water, replace the float with a plastic type. A temporary repair can be made by emptying the float of water, screwing it back on the float arm, and covering it with a watertight polythene bag secured tightly around the float arm with an elastic band.

If the float is not at fault, fit a new washer. Cut off the water supply to the affected cistern if the lavatory cistern is served from the cold water storage cistern. Tie up the ball valve of the storage cistern (see Changing a tap washer) and drain it by flushing the lavatory. If the lavatory cistern is served direct from the mains, or if it is the main cold water storage cistern ball valve that is affected, then it will be necessary to turn off the stopcock situated under the kitchen sink.

Remove the split pin securing the ball valve

BELOW: *Cutaway diagrams showing the component parts of a toilet cistern with an old-style silencer tube* (**Top**) *and a detail of the piston/washer assembly* (**Bottom**) *showing where the washer is secured.*

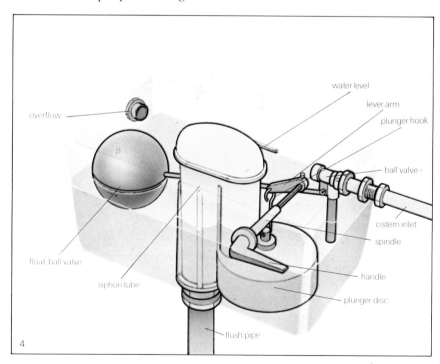

arm (*see diagram 5*) and put both the pin and the ball valve safely to one side. The split pin can break easily when being removed, so have a spare one handy.

Unscrew any cap at the end of the valve case. Insert a screwdriver in the ball arm slot to push out the piston; be ready to catch it as it comes out. At the end of the piston is a screw-on cap which contains the washer. Hold the cap end of the piston in a pair of pliers, insert a screwdriver in the slot and unscrew the cap. Replace the old washer with a new one and replace the screwcap.

If it is difficult to remove the cap, rather than risk a breakage, leave the cap in place and use a penknife to pick out the old washer. The new washer can then be forced under the lip of the cap to rest flat on the seating.

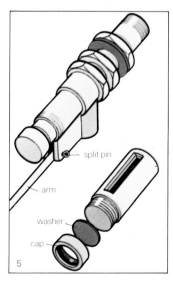

45

Before replacing the piston in the valve body, clean it up with wire wool or fine abrasive paper. Clean inside the valve body and smear the piston with petroleum jelly before replacing it in the valve body. The ball arm can now be refitted.

Leaking cistern If a metal cold water storage cistern starts to leak because of a rust spot, it is best to replace the cistern with a plastic or glass fibre type. The leak can be stopped temporarily by drilling out the hole to enlarge it and plugging it with a cork or tapering wood peg inserted from the inside.

A longer lasting repair, which can also be used on a split, is to patch the cistern using a glass fibre repair kit as for split pipes. The cistern must be drained and the affected part dried and cleaned with a file or abrasive disc in an electric drill.

Lavatory flap valve A lavatory cistern should flush immediately the flushing lever is depressed. If it needs two or three rapid jerks before it flushes, the flap valve needs to be replaced (*see diagram 6*).

The flap valve is a circular plastic disc housed in the siphon. Before dismantling the cistern, buy a new flap valve. Buy the largest you can get and cut it to size with scissors later. It has to cover the plate on which it sits and just touch the walls of the siphon.

To empty the cistern, tie up the ball valve arm and flush the lavatory. Unscrew the nut retaining the flush pipe and disconnect the flush pipe. Use a wrench to remove the large nut immediately below the cistern. Water will flow out, so have a bowl ready.

Above the siphon bell is a metal link that connects the flushing lever to the siphon. Take off this link carefully. Remove the plate from the siphon. Cut the new flap valve to shape and fit it before reassembling the whole system.

Blockages

A blocked lavatory is usually caused by a nappy or similarly large object caught in the waste outlet, or it could be the result of a blockage in the drain outside the house (*see diagram 7*).

A lavatory can be unblocked in the same way as a sink, that is by a sharp downward plunging — in this case with a mop. It is best to have someone standing by at the opened manhole outside to retrieve the blockage as it flows through; if it gets into the drain intercepting trap it may then block the drain.

If the lavatory bowl fills higher than usual when flushed and then slowly subsides to its normal level, there is a blockage in the outside drain. This can be checked by seeing if water is overflowing from gulleys or manholes.

The site of a blockage can be checked by raising the manhole covers. First try the nearest one to the bathroom; when the drains are working properly, this is empty. If it is flooded check the manhole nearest the front garden boundary. If this is empty, the blockage is in the pipe leading from the first manhole to the second. If the second manhole is also flooded, the blockage is between the manhole and the sewer.

To clear a drain blockage you need to hire a set of drain rods. These rods are joined together by screwing them clockwise. It is important to remember this: whether joining rods together, twisting them into the drain or withdrawing them, always turn them clockwise. If you turn them in the opposite direction, they will separate and several sections could be left in the drain. There are three different rodding arm heads: a 100mm (4in) drain plunger, a corkscrew head and a scraper head. A plunger pushes out a blockage, and a corkscrew pulls it out.

Having fitted the correct head and screwed together sufficient rods, probe with the rods in the manhole to feel for the half channel at the base. If you are working from the manhole nearest to the house and the blockage is detected after only a couple of rods have been fitted and pushed into the drain, it is usually more effective to withdraw the rubbish with a corkscrew head.

The blockage is often found in the intercepting trap. Fit the plunger head and feel for the half channel at the base before adding more rods. When the plunger drops into the intercepting trap plunge sharply with the rods until the blockage is cleared.

Sometimes the stoneware stopper of the rodding arm becomes dislodged and falls into the normal outlet below, causing a partial blockage. Water can still escape down the rodding arm but sewage will not and it builds up in the base of the chamber causing a foul smell.

The stopper can be dislodged easily enough to allow the drains to clear. Prevent a recurrence with a lightly cemented piece of slate fixed over the rodding arm hole. The slate can always be broken for future access.

Central heating and radiator repairs

Corrosion in central heating Cold areas in radiators indicate that black iron oxide sludge has accumulated in the radiators as a result of internal corrosion. This can be checked by draining a radiator to see if a thick, black liquid flows out.

Another sign is the need for continual venting of one or more radiators. When venting, hold a lighted taper to the air as it escapes. A jet of blue flame indicates hydrogen gas, a product of corrosion.

It is best to flush the system through completely and to add a corrosion inhibitor. Corrosion inhibitors are available from builders' and plumbers' merchants. A gallon is the usual amount required.

To flush the central heating system, first connect a length of hose to the boiler draincock and run the other end to an outside gulley. Open all control valves; radiator hand valves, the cylinder shut off valve and any others. Open the boiler draincock. Water will flow out and should be replaced at the same rate in the feed and expansion tank in the loft. If the water in the tank falls, adjust the flow of the draincock to restrict the water flow until the tank water remains at a constant level.

During the flushing, tap all over each radiator with a padded mallet to loosen any sludge adhering to the sides of radiators, working from the one farthest from the draincock.

About 20 minutes of flushing is sufficient after clear water first flows from the hose.

Next, tie up the ball valve in the feed and expansion tank until the water level drops sufficiently to allow the corrosion inhibitor to be poured in. Now, most important, turn off the boiler draincock before adding the inhibitor to the tank. Untie the ball valve and return it to its normal position. To ensure that the fluid circulates throughout the system, turn on the circulating pump and allow it to run for half an hour.

With a self-priming system (which has no feed and expansion tank) it is possible to drain down the whole system, disconnect a radiator and pour the inhibitor into it using a funnel, before reconnecting and refilling the system.

Radiator leaks A leaking compression joint can often be sealed by tightening the nut half a turn. If this fails the joint has to be dismantled. Turn off both valves to isolate the radiator from the system and release the nut connecting the valve to the radiator. Some water will pour out so have a bowl and rags ready. Dry off all connections and smear them with joint sealing compound. Reassemble the joint and turn on the valves.

If water is trickling from the point where the pipe enters the radiator, uncouple the joint as before. A hexagon wrench is needed to remove the pipe from the radiator. Dry and clean the thread on the pipe and the radiator, then bind

the male thread with p.t.f.e. sealing tape. Refix the pipe tightly into the radiator using the hexagon wrench.

If the leak occurs on the feed pipe to the valve the system must be drained, after tying up the ball valve in the feed and expansion tank (see Corrosion in central heating, above). If a corrosion inhibitor has been added to the system, collect the water as it drains out and use it to refill the system. Release the nut on the joint, smear sealing compound on the olive and reassemble the joint (see under Burst or split pipes, page 43).

A leaking radiator indicates extensive corrosion inside the system. A leak sealing liquid is introduced into the system via the feed and expansion tank. The liquid finds leaks as it circulates and blocks them up effectively. This liquid will cope only with minor problems.

Special leak sealing compounds are also available for application to the outside of a radiator.

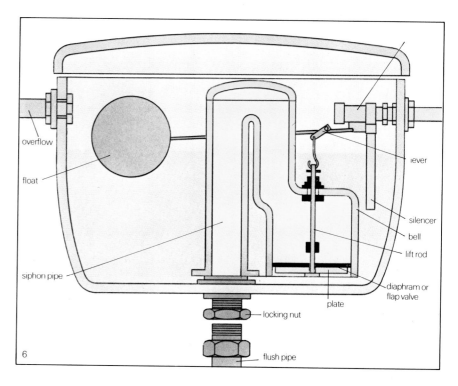

6

overflow

float

siphon pipe

locking nut

flush pipe

lever

silencer

bell

lift rod

diaphram or flap valve

plate

ABOVE: When replacing a flap valve, the entire cistern has to be dismantled. To do this, unscrew the nut retaining the flush pipe, and disconnect the pipe. The large nut immediately below the cistern is removed with a wrench.

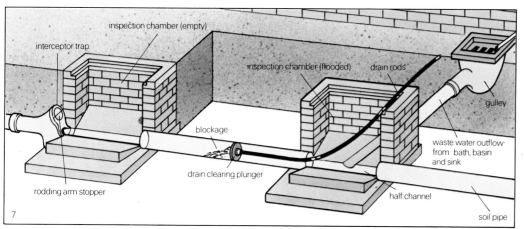

7

inspection chamber (empty)

interceptor trap

inspection chamber (flooded)

drain rods

gulley

blockage

drain clearing plunger

rodding arm stopper

half channel

waste water outflow from bath, basin and sink

soil pipe

LEFT: Clearing a drain blockage which has occurred between two inspection chambers. Various attachments are available to cope with different kinds of blockage.

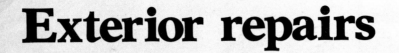

Exterior repairs

With exterior repairs the biggest problem is often presented by the weather. If stripped woodwork has to be left overnight, cover it up with plastic sheets as best you can. Never paint when there is a suggestion of damp on the work or when there is mist about. Also avoid painting in direct sunlight.

The other important point to watch, as indeed with all repairs, is safety. Never take chances by using unsuitable equipment or by stretching just that little bit farther. If you have not got the right equipment, such as ladders or a tower scaffold, then borrow or hire them; the cost of hire is minimal compared with the costs of even a minor accident.

Do be careful when borrowing — inspect equipment carefully for faults and be especially suspicious of painted ladders.

Some of the materials and tools needed when dealing with exterior repairs.
Left to right: *rainwater pipes, tiles, Warrington hammer, galvanised nails, gutter brackets and fittings, slates and a slate ripper for cutting through nails securing slates to battens.*

Roofs

Although they differ greatly in shape and size, domestic roofs all have the same basic construction. There are rafters to which are nailed battens, on which fit slates or tiles which keep the water out. There are flashings for the joints between slates/tiles and adjacent brickwork and there are gutters and downpipes which take rainwater away to the nearest drain.

Water penetration is the most likely trouble to be met with and this can be caused by broken or slipped slates (or tiles), damaged flashings and faulty rainwater fittings. If there is a chimney on the roof, the pointing of the brickwork can fail and the chimney pots with their associated flaunching (mortar base) can crack and fall away.

Access is a problem with roofwork, but with the right equipment (which can be hired from local hire shops) all these troubles can be dealt with by a competent handyman.

Safety

Safety is of paramount importance — see pages 87-89. Never work on any type of pitched (sloping) roof without a roof ladder, and make sure that the ladder or scaffold tower used to get to the roof is securely tied to the building.

Never walk directly on slates, tiles or any kind of corrugated roof; always use crawling boards which will spread the load over a wide area.

It is usually safe to walk on a flat roof covered with roofing felt or asphalt, but never place the foot of a ladder on this type of roof without standing the ladder on a wide, thick board.

Rest boards across several glazing bars when working on a glass roof, and make sure the bars will take the weight without bending. It is best to remove glass for maintenance work.

three rung overlap

one quarter of height

1. *Secure ladder to ring bolt in fascia board. Pad stiles to protect paintwork.*

2. *On soft ground rope ladder to stake and support stiles on a board.*

3. *On uneven base secure one of the stiles with added packing under leg.*

4. *On hard ground use heavy sack of sand or similar ballast to support.*

5. *Slope of ladder: for every 4m height the foot is 1m away from the wall.*

flaunching

flashing

ridge tile

ridge

down pipe

gutter

slate

hip

hip tile

valley

batten

underfelt

fascia

soffit

strut.

rafter

tie or ceiling joist

wall plate

Chimney stacks and pots

Chimney stacks are generally exposed to the elements and are therefore liable to erosion by wind and rain. Pointing between bricks is one possible fault area (see Repointing brickwork page 54). Chimney pots and flaunching (the mortar base into which the pots are set) also suffer from the combined effects of heat, wet, wind and smoke.

A badly cracked pot *can* be repaired, but once you are up on the roof, it is far better to replace it with a new one.

Do take care when removing the old one; a broken portion can be very heavy and to drop it from roof height can be disastrous.

It is essential to remove all the old flaunching with a hammer and cold chisel, carefully placing the debris in a bucket as you work. Make good any of the loose bricks around the top of the stack before positioning the new pot and bedding it on a 3 to 1, sharp sand to cement mix which is sloped all around the pot away to the edges of the stack.

Gutters and downpipes

Blockages Block the downpipe inlet with rags and scrape debris from the gutter with a builder's trowel or a piece of hardboard cut to fit the shape of the gutter. If the downpipe is blocked lay a sheet of polythene under the outlet to catch the rubbish which can be pushed down the pipe with a length of stiff wire, a bamboo cane, or a drain clearing device such as the Sanisnake which can be hired.

With most plastic rainwater systems, the swan neck lifts out of the downpipe, making it easier to clear obstructions.

To prevent future blockages, fit a cage into the entrance of the downpipe. This can be made with a ring of plastic mesh or wire netting wedged into the downpipe inlet. Or you can buy gutter guards which are wire mesh grids which clip along gutters and keep out leaves.

Cracked downpipe Repair temporarily by binding with a waterproof mastic tape, or wrap it with a piece of self-adhesive flashing strip.

Cast iron and asbestos-cement downpipes can be repaired permanently using a glass fibre repair kit (see Burst or split pipes, page 43).

Ideally, all cracked downpipes should be replaced with a new plastic system. In most cases existing metal gutters can be run into plastic downpipes.

Downpipe repairs Loose joints may cause damp patches on walls. Repack these joints with mastic or a putty suitable for metal window frames.

If the downpipe has come loose, refix it to the wall with chisel-point stack-pipe nails which are driven into wood plugs fitted in holes in the brickwork. Alternatively use zinc plated screws driven into wall plugs.

Cracked gutters It is better to replace cracked plastic and asbestos-cement gutters with new sections. To make a temporary repair, clean the inside of the gutter with a wire brush, wipe dry, then fix a patch of metal-backed self-adhesive flashing strip over the crack. Alternatively, patch with foil-backed waterproof mastic tape or cooking foil embedded in thick bituminous mastic compound.

Metal gutters can be repaired in a similar fashion, but in this case treat the inside of the gutter with a rust-killing metal primer after brushing. A long-lasting repair to a crack in a metal gutter can be made using glass fibre filler paste. After making repairs to metal gutters, apply two coats of bituminous paint to the inside.

Holes in gutters Make temporary repairs as described for cracks, but replace with plastic gutters as soon as possible as corroded gutters may fall and are dangerous.

Cast-iron ogee-style gutters are prone to corrosion around the screw holes at the back of the gutter. Drill new fixing holes away from the rusted portion which is then repaired as a crack. Refix the gutter with galvanised mushroom-head gutter fixing screws.

Loose gutter brackets These can cause a length of guttering to sag, leading to joint leaks. If the bracket fixing screw holes have become enlarged, move the bracket to one side and refix. Brackets showing signs of corrosion should be replaced. While the job is carried out give temporary support to the gutter by driving two large nails into the fascia under the gutter. Hold the gutter in the right position with timber packing strips between the nails and the gutter, and refix the brackets.

Leaking gutter joints A satisfactory repair can be carried out on metal gutters by raking old putty out from the joint and injecting in its place a non-setting mastic of the type applied with a mastic gun.

A more reliable method of curing a joint leak is to separate the gutter sections. Cut through the fixing nut and bolt with a hacksaw. Clean away the old jointing material, apply a thick bed of non-hardening mastic or metal window putty and clamp the gutter sections together with a galvanised nut and bolt.

When the gutter sections are replaced, make sure there is a slight fall to the outlet. Use a tightly stretched length of string and a spirit level to get the fall right.

Half-round gutters are supported on brackets and these should be fitted in a line to the fascia board before the gutter sections are clipped into them and bolted together.

Ogee-section metal gutters are screwed direct to the fascia. Be particularly careful to treat the backs of the gutters with rust-resisting metal primer before the sections are replaced. Rest the

LEFT: *Diagram showing how the roof is constructed, and details of its various components. The internal timber work shows all likely constructions. Most roofs do not require such a complex structure.*

barge board

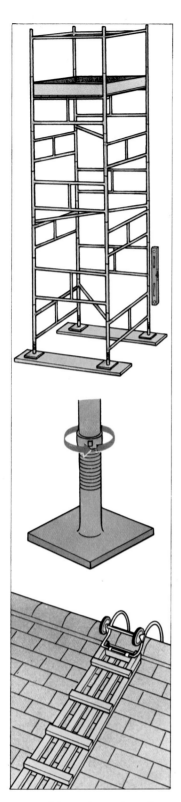

ABOVE: *Safety equipment for scaling roofs. A scaffold tower* (**Top**) *and detail of base* (**Middle**)*, a roof ladder for tiled surfaces* (**Bottom**)*.

first section in the downpipe outlet and fit the remaining sections from this point, using a spirit level to maintain an even fall on the outlet.

If the joints of plastic gutters leak, make sure the sections are properly clipped together. If the leak persists, release the joint and check the sealing gasket. Replace it with a new gasket or use three strips of mastic sealing compound.

Repairs to slates and tiles

Replacing a loose slate Sometimes it is possible to secure a slate without going on to the roof. If the roof is unlined and the underside of the slates can be seen from the loft and the loose slate has slipped only a little way out of place, it is often possible to hook it back into place from the loft.

Bend a piece of stout copper or galvanised steel wire to form a hook. Turn the hook sideways and pass it down the roof under the displaced slate. When the hooked end is clear of the slate, twist the wire until the hook is upright and pull back the wire until the hook catches on the lower edge of the slate. Continue to pull the wire, guiding the slate back into place until its top edge rests on its timber batten. The free end of the wire can then be hooked over a convenient batten and the surplus cut off, giving a permanent repair (*see diagram 1*).

For extra security, before pulling the slate right back into place put two blobs of a gap-filling adhesive on the underside of the slate along the top edge. When the loose slate is pulled into position the adhesive will be sandwiched between the slate and its supporting batten, holding them firmly together.

It will be necessary to climb on to the roof to carry out the replacement of a slate if it has slipped right out of place, if it is broken or missing, or if the underside of the roof is lined. A properly secured roof ladder, or crawling board, will be required.

Secondhand replacement slates can be bought from demolition contractors and some builders' merchants. Most builders' merchants sell new slates and cheaper imitation slates. There are many sizes, so make sure new slates are large enough. If necessary they can be cut to size. The neatest way is to saw them, using a masonry cutting disc in an electric circular saw. Alternatively, gently chop along the cutting line with the edge of a builder's trowel.

Fix the slate into position using a strip of lead, zinc, copper or aluminium about 25mm (1in) wide and 230mm (9in) long. The strip is fixed with a rustproof roofing nail or a galvanised clout nail driven into the gap between the two slates in the row beneath, and into the batten to which these lower slates are nailed.

The new slate is eased into place and the end of the protruding metal strip is bent up to form a hook over the lower edge of the slate.

When a group of several slates is to be refixed, fix the lower slates first with rustproof roofing nails driven through the fixing holes to the wooden supporting battens. Only the uppermost row of slates will need clips.

Cracked and broken slates Cracked slates can be repaired temporarily with a non-hardening mastic gap sealer which is applied along the gap in a narrow bead using an applicator gun.

Alternatively, spread a bituminous mastic compound over the cracked area, lay over the repair a strip of aluminium cooking foil, thin roofing felt, or canvas and top with another layer of bituminous mastic.

Cracked and broken slates are best replaced with new slates. Parts of the damaged slate still held by the securing nails must first be removed using a tool called a slate ripper.

The barbs of the slate ripper are hooked around each securing nail in turn and the handle of the ripper is given a sharp downward pull to cut through the nail and release the slate (*see diagram 2*). A new one is fixed as described above.

Replacing broken and missing tiles Tiles are usually held in place with two small projections at the top, called nibs, which hook over timber battens. Some tiles are secured by nails.

The tiles in the row above a broken tile must be held up with wedges of wood while the nibs of the broken tile are eased over the batten and the damaged tile removed. A builder's trowel will be helpful for lifting the adjoining tiles.

If the tile is held with nails it may be possible to release it by moving the tile from side to side or by easing the nails out with the trowel. If this fails, the nails must be cut with a slate ripper.

Fix the replacement tile by lifting the lower edges of the tiles in the row above and push the tile up until the nibs slip over the batten. A nibless tile can be held with a gap-filling adhesive.

Repairing a snow guard

Refix wire mesh broken away from the support brackets with a twist of galvanised steel wire. If the guard has corroded, replace it with a new strip of galvanised steel mesh fixed to the roof side of the supports.

Straighten support brackets which have been bent by the weight of snow using as a lever a length of steel tube which fits over them. Make sure that ladders you work on are firmly tied to the building and that you have a firm grip on something solid, like a roof timber. For complete safety, work from a scaffold tower cantilevered over the roof which the snow guard is protecting.

If brackets are loose or new ones are required, it may be necessary to remove a few slates or tiles to screw the brackets to the rafters. Replace the slates or tiles afterwards.

Repairs to flashings, valleys and chimney back gutters

Mending flashings Metal flashings are tucked into a mortar joint where the brickwork adjoins the roof. If the flashing comes away from the joint, rake out the old mortar, tuck the flashing back, temporarily holding it in place with scraps of lead or timber wedges and fill the joint with new cement mortar.

Torn and cracked flashings should be thoroughly cleaned and repaired with patches of self-adhesive metal-backed flashing strip. Alternatively, press a thick mastic into the cracks and reinforce the repair with a strip of kitchen foil or thin roofing felt. Finally, overpaint the entire flashing with liquid bitumen proofing.

Flashings in very bad condition should be replaced. The easiest types to fit are self-adhesive metal backed flashing strips which are available in bright aluminium and lead-coloured finishes. To ensure good adhesion, thoroughly clean the area and apply a special primer before pressing the flashing strip into place. Full instructions come with the flashing strip.

If the flashing is a cement fillet it may have cracked and come away from the wall. If the damage is not severe, seal the gap with a non-hardening mastic. If the fillet is in bad condition, replace it with a self-adhesive flashing strip.

Mending valleys and chimney back gutters Small holes and cracks are repaired as described for metal flashings. If the metal valley or back gutter is badly corroded it should be replaced with a sheet of zinc or roofing felt. Surrounding slates or tiles will have to be lifted so the sheet can be taken under them. It may be better to call in a roofing specialist for this major work.

Other types of roof

Repairs to flat roofs These are usually sealed with roofing felt or asphalt. Minor damage can be repaired by applying two coats of a heavy duty liquid bitumen proofing.

If the roof is badly cracked and lifting, roofing felt can be stripped off and replaced. There are usually three layers, plus stone chippings over the surface. Roofing felt manufacturers will supply full fixing details.

The replacement of an asphalt roof should be left to an asphalt and felt roofing specialist.

Repairs to felted shed roofs Sheds usually have a single sheet covering. A small tear can be patched with a new piece of roofing felt stuck down with roofing felt adhesive. Replace a roof in bad condition with sheets of new felt laid along the length of the roof, starting at the eaves (gutters) and finishing at the ridge (*see diagram 3*). Overlap and fix sheets around the edges with 13mm (½in) galvanised clout nails, and secure overlaps with bitumen sealer.

Repairs to corrugated roofs Replace damaged sheets with new ones. Make sure the fixing screws or nails go through the high points of the corrugations.

Small cracks and holes in plastic, metal or asbestos-cement sheets can be repaired by patching with self-adhesive metal backed flashing strip. Alternatively use a waterproof mastic tape.

All types except corrugated plastic can be resurfaced with a heavy duty liquid bitumen proofing.

Glass roof repairs Mend cracked glass and leaks by running a mastic waterproofing tape over the cracks and along the glazing bars. Foilbacked tape lasts longest and is less messy to apply.

If the roof is in bad condition, remove the glass and re-bed it on mastic glazing strip or putty after repainting the glazing bars.

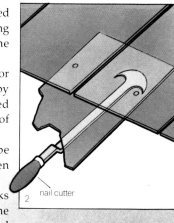

2 nail cutter

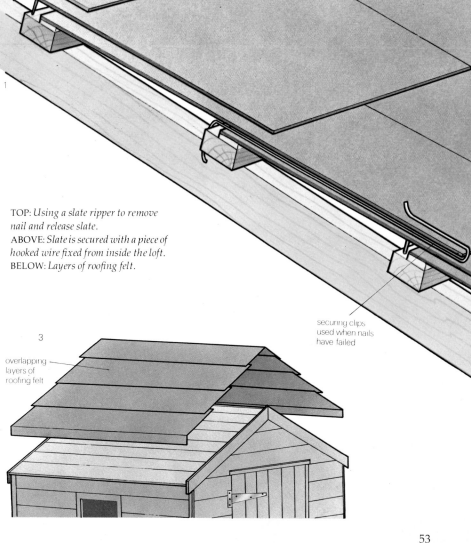

TOP: *Using a slate ripper to remove nail and release slate.*
ABOVE: *Slate is secured with a piece of hooked wire fixed from inside the loft.*
BELOW: *Layers of roofing felt.*

securing clips used when nails have failed

3

overlapping layers of roofing felt

Exterior walls

Walls are made of a wide variety of materials but in essence they are put together in much the same way. Brick and stone walls are tough enough to withstand weathering, although sometimes spalling (breaking away of the face of the material) can occur. The weakest part is the joint between the bricks or blocks and repointing these joints is a likely job on an old wall.

For weatherproofing, and sometimes for decorative effects, many walls have exterior facings added, which commonly are of sand and cement in various forms (pebbledash, rendering, Tyrolean finishes) as well as some more modern finishes such as reconstituted stone slabs, timber and plastic cladding. With the exception of plastic cladding, these all suffer from weathering and are likely to need repairing from time to time.

Such jobs are easy enough provided care is taken and you don't rush the job.

Repointing brickwork

Solid mortar joints between bricks keep a wall weather-resistant and attractive. If the existing mortar is crumbling or loose, chip it out to a depth of 20mm (¾in) using a 9mm (⅜in) wide chisel and club hammer, or an attachment fitted to an electric drill. Brush all dust from the joints.

Before repointing a joint, dampen it with water otherwise the bricks will absorb excessive moisture from the mortar and cause it to crack later.

Proprietary mortar can be bought in bags of dry-mixed ingredients to be mixed with water. Alternatively, use a mix of three parts sand to one part cement.

Adding a small amount of plasticiser will make the mortar smoother and more workable. Plasticiser is bought in cans or bottles.

The basic tools for repointing are a hawk, to hold a small amount of mortar while working, and a pointing trowel. Transfer mortar from the mix to the hawk, flatten it down, cut off a wedge-shaped slice with the edge of the trowel and press it into the joints. Complete the vertical joints before filling the horizontal joints and work about 1 sq. metre (1 sq.yd) at a time.

Weathered pointing (*see diagram 1*) Fill the joint slightly proud of the surface. For vertical joints, rest the left-hand edge of the trowel against the inside face of the left-hand brick. Press the right-hand edge flat against the right-hand brick. Draw the trowel downwards to angle the mortar. A trowel or a tool known as a Frenchman is used in conjunction with a straight-edge to clean up the edges neatly (*see diagram 2*). Make the horizontal joints by pressing inwards with the top edge of the trowel while drawing the tool downwards, and then clean up.

Hollow pointing (*see diagram 3*) First fill the joint flush with the surface. Next, using a length of 9mm (⅜in) diameter iron rod drawn through the joint, aim to leave a concave impression in the mortar (*see diagram 4*).

Flush pointing (*see diagram 5*) The trowel is drawn across the mortar to leave it flush with the brickwork (*see diagram 6*). If this proves difficult, rub the filled joint with a narrow batten wrapped in sacking. Be careful not to smear mortar on to the brickwork.

Damaged wall surfaces

Spalling bricks If a brick weathers badly, it can be removed by chopping out the surrounding mortar with a cold chisel and club hammer. Where a brick is removed intact, it may be possible to re-use it by refitting it with the previously hidden face turned outwards. Alternatively a new brick should be fitted.

Dust out the cavity and dampen it. Spread a layer of mortar around the brick and tap it into the cavity using the trowel handle.

Be careful when removing a brick from a cavity wall. Chippings must not be allowed to drop into the cavity or they could form a porous bridge for moisture to cross from the outer leaf of bricks to the inner leaf and eventually enter the house.

If the surface of a brick has only lightly spalled, a reasonably invisible repair can be made by patching with mortar. Colour additives can be used in the mortar to reproduce the shade of surrounding bricks.

To match the appearance of any surrounding textured bricks, cover a wood float with sacking and press this against the mortar after it has started to set.

Pebbledash repairs An area of damaged pebbledash can be patched invisibly only if matching pebbles can be obtained or the wall is to be painted.

Using a cold chisel and club hammer, chop out the existing rendering around the damaged area and brush out all dust. Dampen the cavity with water and then fill with a mix of one part cement to three parts sharp, washed sand.

Flatten the rendering with a wooden float to bring it flush with the existing surface. While the rendering is still wet, throw on matching pebbles so that they are well bedded in. It may be necessary to press in lightly with a float or piece of board. Leave to set before painting.

If an extensive area of pebbledash has to be renovated, it is worth considering a system introduced by the Blue Circle group. This produces an excellent pebbledash effect using Sandtex, Snowcem and related products. Stockists of these products should be able to provide full details of the system.

Damaged rendering Small cracks should first be undercut, that is, a knife should be drawn down the crack to form a wider cavity behind the surface crack. In effect a V-shaped cavity is formed with the point of the V appearing as the crack on the inner surface (see Hairline cracks, page 18).

Dust out the cavity and dampen it with water. Fill the crack with a suitable exterior grade filler or mortar mix (see Pebbledash repairs, above) applied with a filling knife.

Bulging rendering indicates that it has separated from the brickwork behind. Test suspect areas by tapping lightly with a hammer.

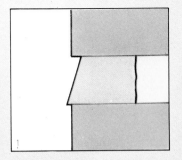

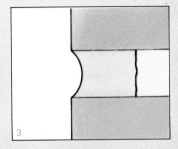

ABOVE: *The most common kind of pointing is called 'weathered'.*
RIGHT: *Remove excess mortar with a pointing trowel.*

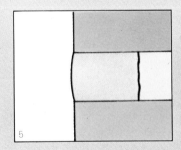

ABOVE: *Hollow pointing is extremely simple to do.*
RIGHT: *Use a bent iron bar 10mm in diameter for hollow pointing.*

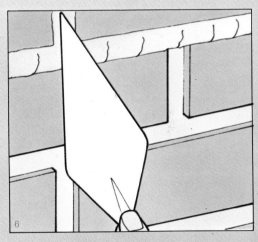

ABOVE: *Flush pointing is used on rendering or painted work.*
RIGHT: *Finishing off flush pointing with a trowel.*

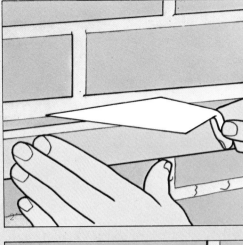

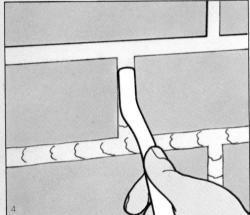

Solid areas will give a solid sound, defective areas will either crack or give a hollow sound.

All loose or cracked material must be hacked out. Any exposed or crumbling brickwork joints should also be hacked out (see Repointing brickwork).

Refill the joints and the rendering using a fresh rendering mix. It is not economical to use proprietary filler for large repairs.

Large areas of fine crazing sometimes occur on rendering. A brush applied slurry of one part cement to one part sand can be worked into the crazing and allowed to dry before repainting the wall.

Smaller crazing problems can be covered by

OPPOSITE: *For most brickwork jobs you will need bricks, cement, buckets and brush, pointing and laying trowels, string line and a level.*

7. *Raking out defective sealing between the wall and window frame.*
8. *Filling the gap with a non-setting mastic.*

painting with good quality masonry paint.

Tyrolean repairs The Tyrolean material is supplied in bags with the ingredients ready-mixed. Various colours are available. Water is added to the mix according to the instructions and the material sprayed on to the wall with a special applicator.

Hack off the existing, damaged finish. Dampen the wall with water and brush on a slurry of Tyrolean finish to serve as an undercoat. Three subsequent coats are needed until the patched area is flush with the surrounding surface.

Each coat should be applied from a different angle so that an all-over covering is built up. Keep the spraying machine at the same distance from the wall throughout the process.

Allow each coat to dry before applying the next. Drying time depends on the absorbency of the wall and the weather. If lightly sprayed with water, the final coat will harden more quickly.

Gaps around window and door frames

These are caused by normal expansion and contraction of the frame and wall. The gap can allow moisture to seep behind the frame causing rot or rust, and possibly damage to internal wall plaster.

Normal fillers are not suitable for sealing the gap as the regular movement of the frame and wall will cause these to crack quickly.

First rake out old gap filler (*see diagram 7*) and dust out the gap with a paint brush. Then use a mastic compound, which remains flexible and will expand and contract with the gap to keep it permanently sealed. Mastics are supplied in tubes with special nozzles or in applicator guns. Run a strip of mastic down the gap (*see diagram 8*). Success in painting over mastic is not guaranteed; although the mastic itself will not be affected, it can push the paint film off.

For improved appearance and to provide a suitable base for paint, a thin strip of timber moulding can be fixed over the mastic with rustless screws.

Repairs to sills and steps

Tiled sills Repairing chips in a tiled sill is possible but the repair will be evident unless it is painted over. Proprietary exterior fillers can be rubbed smooth and flush with the surface when dry.

Replacing a damaged tile with a new, matching tile is the best solution. Use a bolster chisel and club hammer to chop out the damaged tile taking care not to damage surrounding tiles, and chip out the original bedding mortar.

To fix the new tile, use a mix of one part cement to three parts sand. Wet the new tile in water and allow it to drain. Dampen the fixing area on the sill.

Lay a bed of mortar, thicker than for neighbouring tiles and tap down the new tile until it is flush with the surface. Use the handle of the trowel as a lightweight hammer. Excess mortar that squelches out from below the tile can be used to point the joints.

Where a tile has lifted straight off the bedding mortar, damp seeping below the tile is probably causing the trouble. Chip out the original bedding mortar and refix the tile on new mortar (as above) to which a waterproof agent has been added.

For extra protection against damp, paint the sill and its underside.

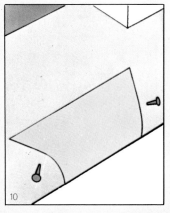

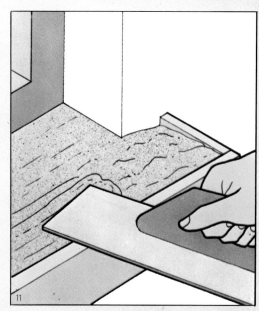

9. *A defective piece of window sill is removed and a new piece cut to fit.*
10. *The new piece is fitted into position using a waterproof glue and rustless nails.*

11. *With concrete sills a new surface is trowelled into place using a framework of battening as a guide.*

Timber sills These will invariably rot if not protected with a sound coat of paint or wood preservative.

Cut out areas of rotting wood working back to sound, dry material. Exterior grade wood filler or general purpose filler suited to outdoor use on timber can be used to fill small indentations, cracks or crevices. Sand the dried filler flush with the surface. Paint the sill, using knotting over resinous patches, primer over bare wood patches, then apply the usual undercoats and top coats.

It is not economical to use proprietary fillers for large repairs. Here, cut out the rotting wood to leave a slightly wedge-shaped cavity (*see diagram 9*). Prepare an infill piece of timber to match closely the shape of the cavity. Apply wood preservative to both the cavity and the infill piece.

Using a gap-filling, waterproof adhesive press the infill piece into the cavity and secure it with rustless screws or nails (*see diagram 10*). Drive nail heads, or countersink screwheads, below surface and fill the holes with exterior filler. Sand smooth when dry and paint the sill.

Keep the drip groove under the sill free from dirt or clogged up paint. This groove prevents damp in the house wall by allowing rainwater to drip off the underside of the sill without reaching the brickwork.

Concrete sills To resurface the sill use a mix of one part cement to three parts sand. Include a waterproofing agent in the mix. Use a cold chisel and club hammer to score the existing surface. Prime the surface with a coat of pva adhesive, diluted according to the manufacturer's instructions. Brush this well into the surface and allow to dry. Pva adhesive improves the bonding of concrete to concrete.

Arrange a framework of battens around the sill to form a mould for the new concrete (*see diagram 11*). Spread a further layer of diluted pva adhesive just before trowelling on the concrete. Smooth out the mix with a steel float used in a circular motion. The top edge of the sill can be rounded off with a steel float when the concrete is set and the batten removed.

Doorsills If a doorsill is badly rotted, complete replacement is the only safe way to prevent accidents to people treading on the sill. For minor repairs to small areas, see Timber sills, above.

Doorsteps Use an exterior grade filler to patch up minor cracks and chips. Allow the filler to dry before rubbing it smooth.

To resurface a badly worn step, first score the top of the surface with a cold chisel and club hammer to provide a key for the new concrete. Brush away all dust and position a framework of battens around the sill to act as shuttering. Heavy weights such as paving slabs or stone blocks can be used to retain the battens. Supporting timber stakes driven into the ground and nailed to the framework are preferable but can be used only where there is earth around the step. Ensure that the shuttering slopes slightly away from the house to allow rainwater to drain off the step.

Prime the concrete with dilute pva adhesive. Immediately before adding fresh concrete, spread another layer of dilute pva on to the step to improve the adhesion of the new concrete to the old.

Make up a concrete mix of one part cement to three parts sand. Fill up the framework until the concrete is just proud of the top edge. Level off the concrete with a timber board on edge resting on the framework. Draw the board towards the front of the step using a chopping motion. Repeat this exercise using a sawing motion. This will leave a slightly rippled, non-slip surface. The step will be usable after three or four weeks.

Paths, gates and fences

Although not strictly part of the house, the surrounding paths, fences and gates must be maintained to keep the whole property in good condition. However well laid, a path or driveway is likely to show signs of settlement in the course of time, and cracks and broken edges are quite common. Driveways are subject to heavy wear from cars and can be damaged not only by physical breaking but by oil and grease stains, which weaken the make-up, especially if the surface is asphalt. And a car jack can make nasty dents in asphalt.

Paving slabs on paths or drives are more vulnerable to damage because the surface is made up of a number of separate units, and the base, or preparation work beneath the finished surface, needs to be even more thorough.

The best base is well rammed hardcore — broken bricks and similar rubble — which is easier to lay properly with an electric compacter, which can be hired.

Fences are frequently made of timber and their exposed positions render them liable to attack by wet, rot and insects. Protection with chemicals helps, but any obvious damage should be put right immediately.

Gates need similar care and suffer from the added hazard of being constantly opened and closed and being ideal playthings for swinging children!

Paths

Repairs to concrete paths

Cracks If the cracks have not worsened for a year or so, they have probably settled and can be repaired safely. Use a bolster chisel and club hammer to undercut the crack (see Damaged rendering, page 55, for technique). Dampen the area and refill the crack with a mix of one part cement to three parts sand. Bring the repair flush with the surface.

Any newly developed cracks are best left for a few months until the movement stops.

Broken edges Use a cold chisel and club hammer to chisel out the damaged concrete, working back to a stable base. Place a timber board alongside the broken edge, supported by stakes well driven into the ground, to contain the new concrete until it has hardened.

Brush diluted pva adhesive on to the concrete, following manufacturer's instructions. Mix up a batch of concrete using one part cement to five parts all-in aggregate. Add a little pva adhesive to the mix to improve adhesion to the old concrete. Fill the cavity, pressing the concrete well down to the base beside the timber board to avoid leaving air pockets below the surface, a possible reason for the edge breaking away in the first place.

Unevenness Depressions that form in a path, or in a drive or patio, invariably lead to a build-up of puddles in rainy weather. Once you are sure that movement has stopped (this can be ascertained only by observation) the depression can be filled.

Depressions less than 10mm (⅜in) thick cannot be filled without first breaking up the affected area. For depressions greater than 10mm (⅜in) use a mix of one part cement to three parts sand to infill. Add pva adhesive to the mix. An initial diluted coat of pva brushed on to the repaired area and allowed to dry will improve adhesion.

1. When repairing an uneven surface on a concrete path, a tamping board is used to level off the surface.

Some of the equipment used for repair work in the garden. **From left to right:** *gloves and screwdrivers, metal hardware for gate fixtures, new gate, mortar, spade and paving slabs.*

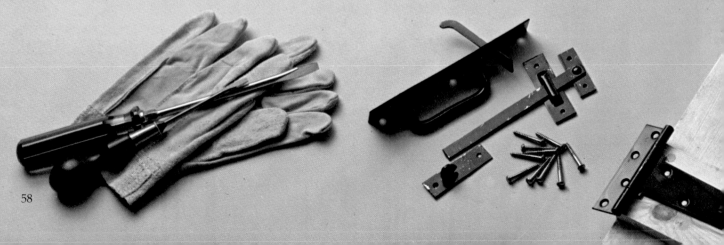

If the depression affects the edge of an area, arrange a support board as for broken edge repairs.

Serious subsidence is caused normally by lack of suitable foundations and the affected area will have to be broken up and the sub-soil filled with well compacted hardcore.

Arrange timber boards on either side of the path with their top edges in line with the surface of the path. Using the same concrete mix as for broken edges, shovel concrete on to the area and rake it level with the existing surface, making sure that no air pockets are left below surface, especially near edges. Finally, place a stout board on its edge across the timber side boards to level off the concrete (*see diagram 1*). Use the

board in a chopping motion on the first pass and a sawing motion on the second.

If the existing path has a slightly rippled surface the fresh concrete should match; allow the new concrete to harden slightly before drawing a stiff broom across the path.

Never tackle concrete repairs in frosty weather as the path is likely to crack as it dries out. Hot weather poses the same problem, but here the fresh work can be protected for a few

days under sacking kept constantly damp with a light spraying.

Do not remove the timber side supports for at least a month, the time concrete takes to dry thoroughly. Removal before a month could leave the edges uncured and liable to break away.

Brick paths

A broken brick can be removed by first tapping it lightly to break the mortar bond below and around the edges. Use a bolster chisel and club hammer and work from the middle outwards. As soon as possible, lift out the pieces with a trowel or similar implement.

The new brick should be laid on a bed of mortar; use a mix of one part cement to three

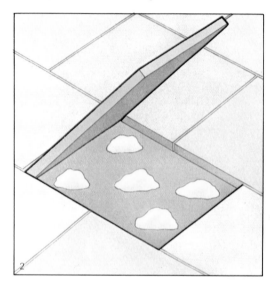

parts sand. Butter mortar around the edges of the brick and place it in the hole. Tap it down level with surrounding bricks with the handle of the trowel.

If the brick will not sink down under light tapping or if it sinks too far, it will have to be removed and the mortar bed adjusted.

Finally, when it is correctly positioned, point the joints (see Repointing brickwork, page 54).

Paved paths

Relaying a paving slab The usual problems with paved paths are caused by subsidence or cracking, both of which necessitate relaying a paving slab. If a slab has subsided, it can often be removed intact and relaid. Prise it up at the edges with a bolster chisel. If it holds firm, break it up with a cold chisel and club hammer, working from the middle outwards. Remove cracked slabs similarly.

To relay the slab or insert a new one use the five-blob method (*see diagram 2*): place a blob of mortar (one part cement to five parts sand) at each corner and one in the middle.

Tap it down, flush with surrounding slabs, using the shaft of the club hammer. Allow two days before filling the joints. At this stage check the level of the stone with a straight-edged length of wood. If necessary, remove it and adjust the base. Brush a dryish mix of sand and cement into the edges and point the joints to suit surrounding slabs.

Asphalt drives

Macadam is available in bags from builders' merchants. If the edge of a drive has broken away, use a bolster chisel and club hammer to cut out a square-sided patch.

To retain the new asphalt until it is solid, place a piece of board alongside the drive, supported by timber stakes. The top of the board should be level with the surface of the drive.

Fill the hole with macadam until it is slightly proud of the surface. Compact it by rolling or tamping with a heavy weight if the patch is small. Remove the support board after 24 hours.

Depressions in the middle of the drive should be square cut as for edges and the hole filled in the same way.

Gates and gate posts

A sagging gate is often caused by a loose post. This can be strengthened with a concrete spur (as for fence posts). It will be necessary to remove the gate if the hinge post is being repaired.

Where the posts are firm and vertical, examine the hinge screws, which could simply need retightening. If the screws fit loosely in the

2. *Laying a paving slab by the five-blob method.*
BELOW: *Cutaway diagram of a garden gate showing how it is mounted on posts set in concrete, and giving details of its component parts.*

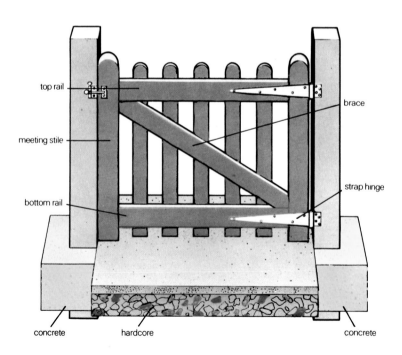

top rail

meeting stile

bottom rail

brace

strap hinge

concrete   hardcore   concrete

holes, remove the hinge and fill the screw holes with timber plugs before refitting the screws. The alternative is to insert longer, thicker screws after drilling larger diameter holes through the hinges.

If the posts and hinges are sound, the gate itself is at fault. The cause will be loose joints throwing the gate out of shape. Galvanized metal brackets can be used to pull loose joints together, although this type of repair might not be visually pleasing. It is preferable to fit strong diagonal braces secured with glue and screws.

Where a lot of joints are at fault, the gate will have to be removed and the weak joints re-made. Mortise and tenon joints are used normally (see diagram 3).

Before dismantling the gate, mark all mating pieces for reassembling the gate in its original form.

Where a tenon is a loose fit in a mortise, saw off the tenon and fill the mortise with a tight fitting piece of timber. Use dowels and waterproof glue to remake the joint.

When repairs are complete and the gate has been reassembled, hold it together with a Spanish windlass until the adhesive has set.

Fences

Fence posts

A fence relies for its strength on strong posts and if these fail it will collapse. Rot is the enemy of timber posts, but it can be controlled by an annual application of a good wood preservative. The most susceptible part of a post is the section buried in the ground and it is worth digging a hole around the base and slapping on a couple of coats of preservative each year.

A rotted base needs strengthening with a concrete spur, available from builders' merchants and garden centres.

Provide temporary support for the post (see diagram 4). Saw off the affected part of the post, cutting back to sound, dry material. Soak the end grain of the post in preservative.

Dig out a hole for the spur and insert it temporarily in the hole to establish its correct position in relation to the post. Mark off the positions for the bolt holes on to the post. Drill the holes in the post.

Reinsert the spur in the hole and ram rubble around it to hold it vertically while the hole is filled with a dryish concrete mix of one part cement to five parts coarse aggregate. Use a spirit level to check that the post is vertical (see diagram 4). Allow the concrete time to set before bolting the spur to the post.

Capping post tops Posts can also rot from the top downwards. Saw off the tops at an angle, cutting out any rotten wood in the process. Rainwater will now drain off the top.

Adding a capping material gives complete protection. Use a piece of zinc or aluminium, folding its edges around the post and securing it with aluminium or galvanized nails (see diagram 5).

Alternatively, cut the post tops square and fit wooden capping pieces (see diagram 6). Soak the capping pieces and the post top in preservative. Secure the caps with aluminium or galvanized nails or screws.

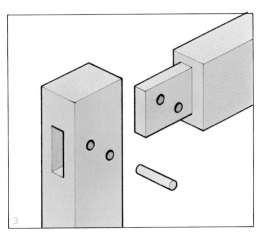

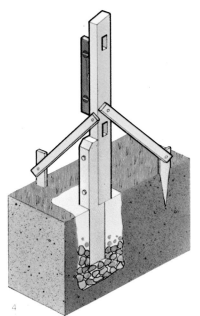

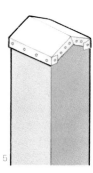

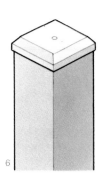

3. A pinned mortise and tenon joint gives a secure fixing for the garden gate.
4. When replacing a fence post, the new post is held in place with temporary struts while the concrete dries.
5. A fence post with zinc or aluminium capping.
6. Post with wooden capping.

General topics

There are a number of jobs which cannot accurately be described as either interior or exterior jobs. The problems caused by damp and condensation, rust, wet and dry rot, woodworm and household pests are not necessarily confined to the inside or the outside of the house. These subjects have therefore been grouped together in this section.

The key to all these problems is, first and foremost, recognition. Once you have identified the cause of the problem there is usually something which can be done to cure it. In some cases, following the instructions given in this section, you will be able to put the problem right yourself. In other cases you may decide to refer your problem to the experts.

Damp

Damp is the single largest threat to all houses, especially during prolonged rainy spells, when the house fabric will be subjected to a watery barrage which will find out defects in the house structure and lead to varying degrees of damp problems inside. Moisture rising from the ground completes the all round exterior attack.

A dry, damp-free house is possible only if the rainwater and moisture are kept outside and the domestic water supply is kept inside the plumbing system of pipes and tanks.

If damp does gain a grip it can turn a comfortable home into a miserable place. There will be a stale smell, a dampish atmosphere and clothes and blankets possibly coated with mildew. In short, it will create a generally unhealthy environment.

Dire, expensive faults can develop in the house structure. However, if the problem is recognised and treated at an early stage, the worst that can happen is a damp patch on a wallcovering requiring redecorating after the cause of the damp has been cured.

Damp can be recognised by wet patches on walls, ceilings or floors often immediately traceable to a structural defect in the house.

Not all such wet patches result from damp; the trouble may be condensation, (see page 66).

Wet concrete or stone floors can be diagnosed with a simple test. Place a small piece of glass, say 50mm × 50mm (2 × 2in), on a ring of putty or Plasticine on the floor with the glass bedded firmly on the ring to form an airtight cavity. Leave it for a day or so and then check. If moisture appears below the glass, the floor is damp; if the moisture settles on top of the glass, condensation is the cause.

House construction and damp proofing

Modern houses, particularly many built since the 1920s, are constructed with in-built barriers against damp. Each exterior wall is formed from two leaves of brickwork with a 50mm (2in) air space between. This is called a cavity wall. The inner and outer leaves of bricks are tied together with metal wall ties spaced at regular intervals.

A damp proof course is built into the brickwork near ground level. This damp proof course is constructed from a thin, impervious material laid in the mortar joint between the second or third courses of brick above ground level and is often visible. The material used is either slate or bituminous felt and continues right around the house.

Most ground floors in modern houses are concrete, and incorporate a complete sheet of waterproof membrane that stretches right over the floor and links with the damp proof course of the walls to create a continuous waterproof barrier across the house.

This building method is designed to prevent rainwater soaking through to the inside walls or moisture rising from below ground and attacking the floor of the house or the walls. Unfortunately, this theoretically waterproof design does not function properly in every house because of faults or errors during building.

The 50mm (2in) cavity between the inner and outer leaves of brick may be bridged by moisture if, during building, some mortar drops into the cavity and settles on a metal wall tie. It then forms the ideal porous bridge for any moisture that has penetrated the outer leaf of bricks to cross to the inner leaf. Eventually it will soak through the inner leaf and show itself as a tell-tale damp patch on the wall inside the house.

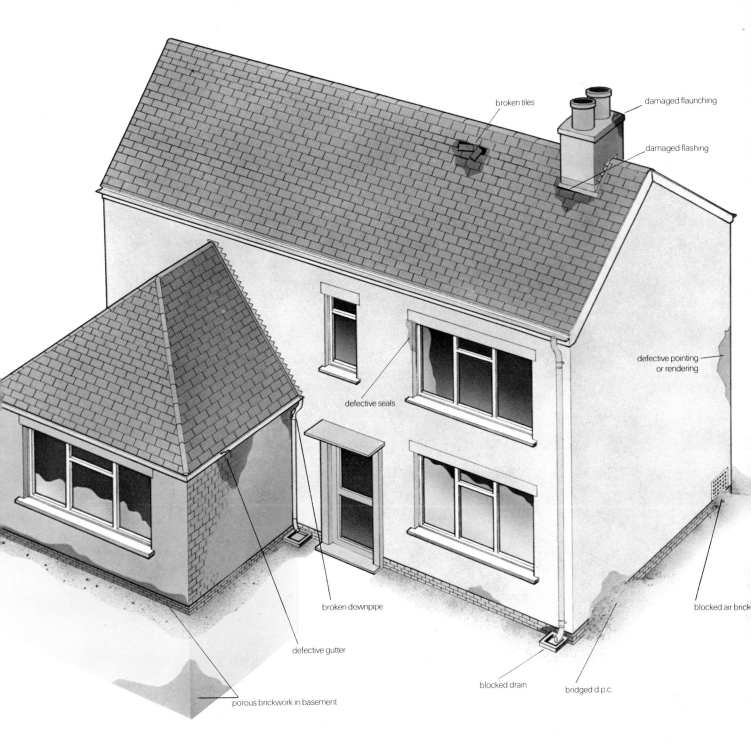

broken tiles

damaged flaunching

damaged flashing

defective seals

defective pointing
or rendering

broken downpipe

defective gutter

blocked air brick

porous brickwork in basement

blocked drain

bridged d.p.c.

Rising damp, that is moisture soaking upwards from below ground, is not a usual problem as the wall and floor damp proof courses normally provide an effective barrier. However, if there is a fault in the floor membrane or in the wall damp proof course, moisture can find its way through.

Older houses did not have damp proof barriers incorporated in the structure. Thick materials were used to prevent moisture creeping through the walls. Ground floors that are of suspended timber construction ventilated by airbricks low down in the walls are normally trouble-free, provided the air bricks are left uncovered. Solid floors rely directly upon thickness to stop damp.

Sometimes the thickness of material proves effective, as any moisture gradually soaking through can dry out again when the weather becomes warmer and more settled. Often, though, the moisture penetrates into the house.

Damp from roofs, chimneys and gutters

With roofs the problems are usually caused by missing slates or tiles, or cracks. Cracks are not easy to identify from the ground, although a pair of binoculars can help. It is better to climb into the loft on a very wet day and spend half an hour looking and listening for drips. You will need a powerful torch to trace any drips back to a crack in a tile or slate; the drip is often some distance from the actual damage.

ABOVE: *Diagram of a typical house showing the likely danger spots for damp, and the probable causes. Check your house regularly, using the diagram as a checklist.*

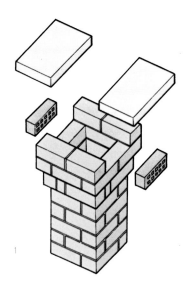

ABOVE: *Capping an unused chimney stack with paving slabs and ventilation bricks. The chimney pots have been removed first.*

Missing or slipped tiles will have to be replaced or repositioned, whereas some cracks can be sealed effectively with mastic or self-adhesive waterproof tape.

Where a roof has weathered extensively it is not feasible to repair individual defects. Here an all-over treatment with a proprietary brush-on waterproofing compound or a system incorporating a damp proof membrane should be used.

A roof that is too badly damaged for any remedial treatment will need a complete recovering.

Driving rain or snow will find gaps under even firmly fixed and sound tiles and slates. These gaps can be sealed effectively with strips of bituminous underfelt. Secure the strips to the rafters with strips of wood pinned in place.

Corrugated roofs also suffer from inblown wind or snow, which can be excluded by fixing specially moulded foam strips to seal the ends of the corrugations.

Where corrugations meet a wall, the join can be sealed with aluminium flashing tape. There are easy to use kits which contain all the necessary materials: primer, mastic and tape.

Detailed roofing repairs are covered in the chapter on Roofs (pages 48-53).

Damp problems with chimneys Where chimney stacks adjoin roofs, flashings are used to seal the chimney brickwork to the tiles or slates. The flashing can become defective or slip out of place, allowing rainwater to seep through the chimney-to-wall joint into the loft.

Damp patches on chimney breast walls are a warning sign of a damaged chimney stack. In extreme cases the stack can deteriorate to the point of collapse — a disastrous, though fortunately rare, occurrence.

A preliminary inspection can be made through binoculars but suspicious areas will need a close-up check, especially a cracked pot, damaged flaunching (that is the sloping bed of mortar in which the pot sits), damaged rendering or mortar joints.

A damp patch on a chimney breast wall is often caused by a blocked up fireplace, where no allowance for ventilation has been made. The covering material should always have a gap left in it to allow for sufficient ventilation, in the form of an airbrick or a hole of about 100mm × 50mm (4 × 2in) cut into the board used.

Damp within a flue can be caused by water vapour given off through burning fuel or waste matter, and a flue liner will cure the trouble. For gas or oil appliances, a metal flexible flue liner should be installed to isolate the water vapour from the chimney walls.

If a chimney is no longer used it can be fitted with a special capping pot which keeps out rainwater but allows adequate ventilation. Alternatively, the chimney pots can be removed and a paving slab bedded across the stack, with space on either side of the stack for an airbrick (*see diagrams 1 and 2*).

Renovating chimneys means working at a height and so safety is essential. You must use either a proper roof ladder, firmly secured to the building or, if the position of the stack allows, a scaffold tower. Most chimney repair jobs are within the scope of the handyman, but rebuilding a stack should be handled by a professional roof repairer.

Damp caused by gutters and downpipes
Overflowing or leaking gutters and downpipes are another source of interior damp problems. Untended gutters will inevitably become blocked with debris and leaves. An annual inspection and clear-out is essential as gutters have been known to collapse under the weight of debris. Usually a blockage merely causes water to tumble over the edges to splash on to the walls. Check the entrance hole to the downpipe, as a bird may have chosen this as a nesting spot, and bring out any obstruction.

Rust, sagging gutters, defective joints are some other common problems. Gutter repairs are detailed in the chapter on Roofs (see page 51).

Damp from exterior walls

Exterior walls are of facing bricks, painted bricks, or cement rendered, pebbledash or Tyrolean finish. A solid, sound rendering, covered with a good quality exterior paint or plastic coating is a generally adequate safeguard against damp. Sound pebbledash or Tyrolean finish also offer excellent protection. All brick walls must have sound mortar joints.

When examining walls, look for cracked, bulging or loose areas of rendering. Any loose material must be hacked away and all cracks filled with a fresh sand and cement rendering.

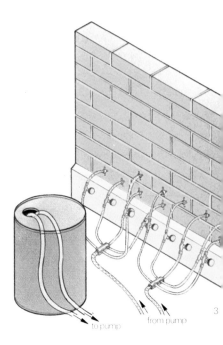

Pebbledash repairs also entail hacking out damaged material and applying a fresh rendering base for new pebbles. Try to obtain pebbles that will match the existing walls. An invisible repair is easier if the wall is to be painted.

An all-over crazing effect often appears on rendering, and is remedied by brushing a slurry of 1 part cement and 1 part sand into the cracks before finishing with a good quality paint.

Inspect the mortar joints between bricks. If these are crumbly and loose, they should be raked out to a depth of 20mm (¾in) and repointed with fresh mortar.

If rainwater penetrates a sound wall, brush on a coat of silicone water repellent. This colourless liquid provides an effective barrier against the rain and allows water vapour trapped in the wall to escape.

When examining the outside walls, check that the air bricks situated near the base are not blocked up. Air bricks must be kept clear at all times to ensure good underfloor ventilation.

Replacing a damp proof course Damp patches situated low down on the interior walls point to a defective, or absent, damp proof course. First make sure there is not something more basic causing the trouble; earth is sometimes piled up against a house wall and extends above damp proof course level. Also, check the level of any paths adjoining the walls; these should be at least 150mm (6in) below the level of the damp proof course. A path that is too high can allow rainwater to splash up constantly above the damp proof course or, in times of heavy rainfall, the path may be turned into a small river, the level of which could remain above the damp proof course for some time.

If a new damp proof course is required, there are various ways to insert one, but only one method is suitable for the competent d-i-y person. This is a chemical barrier, formed in the walls by feeding a liquid through a series of drilled holes made at regular intervals. The liquid can be fed through the wall by pressure injection (*see diagram 3*) which is quicker, or by gravity fed from a series of special bottles lodged in the holes (*see diagram 4*).

The liquid is fed into the wall from the outside and will soak through brickwork up to 225mm (9in) deep to leave an impervious barrier right across the wall.

Often the chemical injection is combined with another method of damp proofing, called the siphonage method. Porous earthenware tubes are fixed into the wall at damp proof course level to slope downwards towards the outside air (*see diagram 5*). The tubes absorb moisture in the wall and cool it, making the air more dense so that it flows outside and is replaced by fresh air drawn in. In effect, air circulation is set up with the tubes acting as a drying medium. The entrances to the tubes on the outside wall are covered with grilles to keep out rainwater.

A physical damp proof course can be installed by another method: a special power saw is used to slice through the mortar courses between two courses of brickwork (*see diagram 6*) and a membrane material is slipped into the saw cut.

Electro-Osmosis is a third method: a copper strip inserted at damp proof course level is linked to earth electrodes in the soil. Minute electric charges in a wet wall are discharged down the link, so preventing the moisture rising in the wall. This damp proofing is beyond the scope of amateurs and has to be carried out by experts.

Damp proofing interior walls

Walls can also be waterproofed from inside by brushing on liquid sealers. This not only cures the damp but prevents it from spoiling decorations.

BELOW: *Various methods of making a damp proof course.*
3. *The best d.i.y. method. A chemical barrier is fed through the walls by pressure injection.*
4. *Alternatively the same effect is achieved with gravity feeding from a series of bottles.*
5. *This method is often combined with the siphonage method, where porous earthenware tubes slope downwards to the outside air.*
6. *A professional contractor will have to be called in to install this kind of damp proof course. A special power saw is used to cut through the mortar courses between brickwork.*

Internal walls can also be lined with waterproof laminated paper or aluminium foil. Some of these will adhere to a damp surface. Many interior treatments contain fungicides which prevent fungal attack, a common result of dampness.

Another, more extreme, measure often used in cellars and basements is to line the walls with a pitch-impregnated fibre base, which is corrugated to form dovetail keys for plastering on one side and has insulating cavities on the other. This material is usually fixed to brickwork or masonry with galvanised nails. Supplied in rolls about 5m × 1m (16ft × 3ft), it is sufficiently flexible to be turned around corners and is easy to cut.

Any damp plaster has to be removed, back to brickwork or masonry. The rolls of material are then fixed with vertical joins overlapped and horizontal joins butted up. To finish, plaster can be applied or panel boards fixed direct to the sheeting with nails or a special adhesive applied to the panel boards in blobs.

Damp from windows

Window defects can be spotted readily. A sound window has a solid, unbroken sheet of glass embedded in sound putty or wood. Check that there are no gaps between the frame and wall where moisture can seep through. These gaps open and close through normal seasonal movement. The same problem can occur with door frames (see page 33).

Below the window sill there should be a drip groove, an indentation running through the complete length of the sill. It is this groove that prevents rainwater reaching the house wall. Keep the grooves free from clogged up paint and dirt — it takes only a few minutes to go right around the house to clear them out. Should a sill not have a drip groove, fit a strip of painted wood beneath the sill to act as a drip groove.

Cracks in glass can be sealed with self-adhesive waterproof tape applied to a clean, dry surface which is also useful around the glazing bars of skylights. Foil covered tapes are longer lasting. An alternative is to remove the glass and replace it on a firm bed of putty or mastic glazing strip.

Defective putty is usually found at the base of the glass. Hack it all out, prime the rebate with suitable wood or metal primer and run new putty along the glass. Use the appropriate type of putty for the frame.

Damp floors

A damp concrete floor can be waterproofed by brushing on a rubberised bituminous emulsion. The floor must first be cleaned by damping and brushing. A water-diluted priming coat is followed by two full coats, allowing drying time between coats. A further coat of the material can

be used as an adhesive for linoleum, vinyl/asbestos tiles or wood blocks.

Pitch epoxy sealers are applied similarly. These are supplied in two parts which are mixed together and applied by brush or trowel. This sealer can be taken up the walls (behind the skirtings) to link with an existing wall damp proof course.

More serious cases require a sandwich treatment. The floor must first be cleaned thoroughly. Two full coats of the material are applied, allowing drying time between coats. While the top coat is tacky, clean, sharp sand is sprinkled over to provide a key for a 50mm (2in) thick floor screed. Again, the damp proofing liquid can be taken up the walls to tie in with an existing damp proof course.

Plumbing

For repairs, see chapter on Plumbing, pages 42-47.

Garden flooding

If a garden floods regularly, except during torrential storms, it may need a drainage system, as garden flooding can affect the house foundations and walls. A land drainage system can be laid using 75mm (3in) diameter perforated pitch fibre pipes. The pipes must be laid to a fall away from the house and be buried 800mm (30in) deep with perforations facing downwards.

Where pipes change direction or meet at a junction, catchpits are handy. Catchpits can be built of brick or stone and fitted with a waterproof cover. Should the pipes become silted up, the catchpits will enable you to locate blockages. They act as gulleys, in effect.

Local authority permission must be obtained for the water to be discharged into the domestic drainage system; a ditch could be a convenient alternative.

A soakaway is an alternative to land drainage. A pit, 1½m × 1½m × 1½m (5ft × 5ft × 5ft), filled with rubble and topped with 300mm (12in) of soil is ideal, though precast concrete soakaways can be bought.

Condensation

Condensation can be a more serious problem than damp. Positive action can be taken to eliminate damp completely, but attempts to cure extreme condensation may not be totally successful.

The marked similarity between damp and condensation often makes it difficult to distinguish between them and this is essential for the correct remedial measures to be taken.

To many people, condensation means misted windows, or beads of moisture, and these specific signs of condensation cannot be confused with damp. However, there is an area of overlap; — of wet patches on walls and ceilings and, in extreme cases, on floors. Here the cause of the problem is less easily defined.

A good day to identify condensation is when the weather is cold and dry and windows start to mist up and stream. If tell-tale wet stains appear on walls or ceilings, the cause is condensation.

A simple test to see if damp or condensation is affecting floors is given on page 62.

To understand the purpose of anti-condensation measures, it is helpful to know what causes it. The air in a house is moistened by normal domestic activities; cooking, washing, bathing, drying laundry, burning unvented gas, solid fuel or paraffin, and by the basic human function of breathing. All these discharge water vapour into the air and raise the room temperature. The warmed air thus becomes heavily laden with water vapour. When this warm, moisture-laden air contacts a cold surface, it condenses.

Preventing condensation

The cure for condensation encompasses a correct balance of heat and ventilation, and proper insulation of cold surfaces.

Much can be done to reduce condensation at source. Most steam is generated in the kitchen and bathroom, but these rooms may not be the worst affected by condensation, as the air temperature in them may be reasonably high, so the water vapour in the air is drawn towards

ABOVE: *Condensation is most easily spotted on window surfaces. It can be very difficult to cure.*

unheated rooms where it condenses on cold surfaces.

Efforts should be made to minimise the creation of water vapour in the kitchen and bathroom: before running hot water into a sink or bath, fill the base with a couple of inches of cold water: never allow saucepans to steam away uncovered or the kettle to boil longer than necessary. Drying laundry indoors is sometimes unavoidable but should be avoided if at all possible. Tumble dryers generate an enormous amount of steam and must always be used with the extraction tube supplied by the manufacturers.

Some thought should be given to the general level of warmth within the house over a 24 hour period. A house that is constantly warm is less prone to condensation than one that is heated only twice each day, a familiar pattern in modern house heating. The house is allowed to become cold overnight and is then heated briefly in the morning. During the day the heating is turned off and the house becomes cold again. The heating is turned on again for a few hours in the evening. Though the two periods of heating raise the air temperature to a comfortable temperature for the family, the house structure never receives enough heat to raise it above dew point level, and there are many constantly cold surfaces for condensation to form upon.

Ideally, the central heating should be left on at a low temperature during the day when the house is unoccupied. Any increase in fuel bills, however justified or small, is rarely acceptable, and this course of action is likely to be taken only when there is an acute condensation problem.

Heating appliances It is important to choose heating appliances carefully. For every pint of fuel used by a paraffin heater, an equal amount of water vapour is released into the air. Unflued gas or oil heaters also boost condensation. The ideal is the dry heat produced by radiators, electric convectors, infra-red tubes or radiant fires.

Extracting moist air Open windows provide adequate ventilation but are not desirable on a cold day; it is far better to install extractor fans or ventilators, which control ventilation.

There are two types of fan. The first is a simple, portable recirculatory fan, which moves the air about to keep it cool. This copes with a minor steam problem if it is positioned to blow steam towards an open window or air brick.

The second, the extractor fan, changes the air and copes with a heavy concentration of steam. There are types for fitting in windows, walls, roof lights, pitched roofs or in a ceiling below a loft.

Some types are single purpose, that is, they suck air out of the room. Reversible flow types are switch operated either to suck air in or blow it out. Some fans have back-draught shutters which close automatically when the fan is switched off to prevent draughts.

To produce the best results a fan must be large enough to suit the size of the room and sited as high up in the room as possible, close to the cooker or other source of steam. If there is a boiler in the room, seek expert advice on the necessary type of fan and its situation. An extractor can starve a boiler of combustion air, leaving dangerous fumes circulating in a room.

Extractors are rated in terms of extraction capacities expressed in cubic feet per hour. To work efficiently, a fan must be capable of producing 15 to 20 air changes per hour in a kitchen, and 6 to 10 air changes per hour in a bathroom. A fan incorporating a variable speed control is useful but it must be capable of coping with the maximum air change figure required in a room.

To calculate the size of fan required, work out the cubic volume of a room in feet and multiply this by the number of air changes required per hour. For example, a room measuring $10 \times 8 \times 8$ft (approx $3m \times 2\frac{1}{2}m \times 2\frac{1}{2}m$) $\times 15$ (air changes) needs a fan with a capacity of 9,600 cu.ft hour (approx $280m^3$ hr). Usually a fan with a 6in (150mm) diameter impeller will suit the average kitchen. An oversize extractor is as bad as an undersize one, as it will draw excessive heat from the room.

Where a fan is fitted in a window, the glass must be strong enough to take it or be replaced with a new sheet of glass. Seek guidance from your supplier, and ask him to cut the hole in the glass for the fan.

A ventilator may be sufficient where a steam problem is minimal. A simple fixed louvre, or hit or miss ventilator set in a wall, window or above a door could be used in conjunction with a recirculatory fan directed at it. The louvre grilles are normally opened and closed with a slide adjuster.

Open fires need an adjustable ventilator, ideally situated on either side of the hearth and fitted in the floor. Obviously this will not be possible with a solid floor, and in such cases the ventilator can be fitted over the door leading to the hall.

There is no hard and fast rule to follow when trying to strike a happy balance between heat and ventilation. Each situation will differ. The homeowner has to establish by trial and error the best way to minimise condensation.

Cooker hoods are an excellent means of removing kitchen steam. There are two types. The first recycles the air through a charcoal filter built in the hood. The second carries the steam through ducting to the outside air. The ducting can be built into the backs of cupboards and so on if a long run is required from the cooker to the outside air.

Finally, if you intend to modernize your home

and block off the fireplace, leave a built-in allowance for ventilation.

Having created a reasonable heat and ventilation balance, attention can be given to insulating cold surfaces and choosing appropriate decorative materials.

Curing condensation

Condensation on walls This can be solved by normal thermal insulation methods. Lining the walls with expanded polystyrene sheeting before decorating will keep them warm and reduce heat losses.

Expanded polystyrene is sold in rolls and in thickness from 2 to 5mm (about 1/16in to 3/16in). It is hung in much the same way as wallpaper.

Really severe cases need a more elaborate and expensive method of thermal insulation. Cavity walls can be filled with urea-formaldehyde foam or mineral wool, which is a job for a specialist company. The whole process takes an average of one day.

Solid walls are far more difficult to insulate thoroughly. The best method is to line the walls with thermal insulating boards fixed to a framework of battens or direct to the wall with nails and special adhesive. This is sometimes a major undertaking, requiring the repositioning of door and window frames, skirtings, plumbing, electric switches and socket outlets.

A simpler alternative is to fix a tubular heater to the base of a cold external wall to keep it permanently warm.

Where mould, mildew or fungus has affected a wall, it must be treated thoroughly before redecorating. Strip off any existing wallpaper and apply a fungicidal wash to the wall.

If walls are to be repapered, choose a washable paper or vinyl wallcovering. Hang these with a paste containing a fungicide.

Special anti-condensation paint also is designed to act as an insulator between the moist air and the surface. The paint also absorbs moisture when the humidity is high and releases it when the air is drier.

Condensation on ceilings Use expanded polystyrene as a base for paper or paint. Polystyrene tiles are a suitable alternative, and are fixed with adhesive. They can be painted with emulsion or fire retardant paint, preferably before being fixed to the ceiling.

Condensation on floors Existing condensation must be eliminated with standard measures. Floorcoverings that provide effective insulation barriers include fitted carpets and decorative wooden flooring in blocks, strips or tiles. For kitchens or bathrooms, cork, sheet vinyl or vinyl tiles with a foamed interlayer or other underlay are ideal.

Quarry tiles can cause condensation problems, which can be treated only by covering the tiles with a floor screed or layer of hardboard, to

form an underlay for one of the coverings stipulated above.

Condensation on windows The only effective cure for chronic condensation is double glazing. Total elimination of misting is possible only with expensive hermetically sealed units. Even with these, in extreme cases, there could still be misting on the room side of the glass.

All other double glazing systems (secondary sashes, coupled windows or d-i-y kits) will reduce the problem in proportion to their quality and efficient installation, which must produce a sealed cavity between the two sheets of glass.

Where the double glazing unit can be opened on hinges or by sliding, any condensation that does form can be wiped away. If this has to be done frequently, the only solution is to drill some holes through the sill to the outside air. The holes should be about 6mm (1/4in) in diameter and plugged with glass wool to keep out insects. The number of holes needed depends on the severity of the problem, and should be assessed by trial and error; start with two and progress from there.

A less effective method is to place a bag of silica gel crystals between the two panes of glass. The crystals absorb the moisture but quickly become saturated and have to be removed frequently to be dried out.

Misting on metal window frames is a persistent problem and difficult to prevent. Some new frames on the market have built-in insulation barriers.

Condensation from plumbing system Boxing-in any pipe runs will cure condensation on them. Do not box-in any pipe runs on outside walls of cold rooms as this will lead to freezing in winter; paint these pipes with anti-condensation paints.

Anti-condensation paint can also be applied to a cistern. If this fails, the inside of the cistern can be lined with expanded polystyrene. Drain the cistern and dry it thoroughly. Fix the polystyrene with epoxy resin adhesive and allow it time to dry before refilling the cistern.

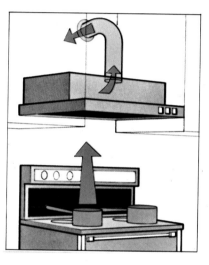

Cooker hoods are an excellent way of removing kitchen steam. There are two main kinds, the recirculating type **(Top)** *and the extractor type* **(Above)**.

Rust

Rust gains a rapid grip on metal and eats its way through it. In some cases, an item that is in good condition in the autumn can be badly affected, possibly beyond the point of repair, by springtime.

Any unprotected metal items will certainly rust if left outside or in a cold, damp garden shed. Simple precautions will prevent rust and obviate the extensive effort and expense of removing it.

In essence, rustproofing prevents air and moisture from contacting metal surfaces. Rust attacks only iron and steel. Affected metals undergo a chemical change and return to their original form, iron oxide.

There are a whole host of rust prevention products sold under various brand names. Rust binding metal primers have special pigments which inhibit rust formation.

Prevention

Any iron or steel that is suitable for painting should first be treated with a brush coat of rust-inhibiting primer. Follow with normal undercoat and use gloss paint to finish. A solid film of paint is important to prevent water vapour finding its way through tiny cracks in the coating and setting up corrosion. When the paint film on metal is seen to blister, the cause will almost certainly be a sub-surface rust attack.

If metal items cannot be painted, cover them with a good coat of oil. Oil tends to evaporate quickly out of doors and any metal items being stored in the garden should be protected with grease.

Should the garden shed be uninsulated or unheated, it is worth while bringing all tools inside the house during winter. If this is not possible, smear all metal parts with a healthy covering of grease before putting tools away for the cold months. Cupboards, drawers or sound boxes make the best storage places. Leave lids or doors slightly open so that air can circulate. As an extra precaution, place special rust-inhibiting paper next to the tools.

An excellent insurance against rust is to insulate the shed thoroughly and warm it with a greenhouse-type heater to maintain an even temperature.

Seal outdoor hinges and latches with grease, but not the front gate, as visitors will not want sticky fingers!

Any new metal items being fixed in permanent positions should first be protected with rust-inhibiting primer and normal paint coats. Screw and bolt threads should be dipped in Vaseline before being inserted. They will twist out much more easily if they have to be removed.

Gutters must always be well maintained with a sound coat of paint, either gloss or bituminous. Replacement gutters should be plastic types, which will never corrode.

Inside the house, a likely area of rust trouble is in the water storage tank in the loft. The simplest way to prevent corrosion here is to suspend a sacrificial anode in the water (*see diagram 1*). Only the anode will waste away and not the galvanising on the tank which protects the tank body from rust. In other words, the anode is sacrificed, hence its name. Should the tank ever need to be replaced, choose a plastic type.

If the tank is still in good condition, alternative preventative measures are to drain the tank dry and insert a plastic liner or apply a couple of coats of taintless, odourless bitumen paint.

The only other area of likely trouble inside the house is a wet central heating system. Corrosion here can be prevented or halted with corrosion inhibitors (see page 46).

Treatment

When corrosion is discovered, all rust must be removed back to bare metal, which must be well cleaned. Small spots can be cleaned away with emery paper; larger areas need to be wire brushed by hand or, much easier and quicker, a wire cup brush fitted to an electric drill. Wear goggles to protect the eyes from flying particles. To finish, rub down the surface with abrasive paper. Surrounding metal that has not yet rusted should be cleaned thoroughly to remove all dirt and grease.

No matter how thoroughly cleaned metal appears to be, there is always the possibility that minute particles of rust will remain on the surface. To dissolve these or render them inert, apply a chemical neutraliser, and brush rust inhibiting primer all over the surface, making sure that screw heads, rivets and edges receive a good coating. To finish, paint with undercoat and gloss.

Where it is not possible to dismantle items to clean and treat them properly, remove as much rust as possible before applying a rust-inhibiting primer. These are available in aerosol form for spraying otherwise inaccessible areas.

Rusty gates and railings can be cleaned more easily with a blowlamp and scraper to remove old paint and corrosion. Use a shavehook to clean out cracks and crevices. Treat with chemical neutraliser and rust-inhibiting primer before normal painting.

If items have to be dismantled and nuts, bolts or screws have locked solid, tightening the fixing a little will sometimes break the rust grip. If this fails, it is because the rust has locked the whole assembly rigid. Rust release fluids are available which often work but need time to do

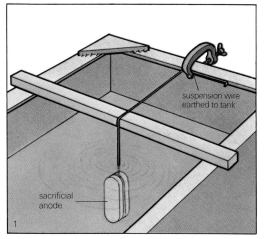

their job. Apply a few squirts and try loosening the fixing later.

Another possibility is to heat the head of the fixing device with a soldering iron, to expand the metal and break the rust grip.

Rust in a water tank requires immediate attention: 250 litres of water pouring through the ceiling is not an attractive proposition.

To treat recent corrosion, empty the tank and remove loose or flaking rust by wire brushing. Apply a rust inhibiting liquid to neutralise any rusted areas. Small holes can be filled with epoxy resin filler. Allow the filler time to harden before brushing on a couple of coats of bitumen paint. When dry, the tank can be refilled.

While the tank is empty, it is worth while checking the pipework holes made in the walls and base. This entails temporarily dismantling pipes to clean the holes and coat them with bitumen paint, but it is time well spent.

Metal windows require the normal treatments; cleaning, rust inhibitor, primer and normal paint coats. Alternatively, paint the cleaned frames with cold galvanizing paint. This zinc-rich paint will kill the rust action. Follow with normal painting.

Rusted gutters or downpipes can cause damp inside the house. Clean out any debris before removing any rust. Holes or cracks can be filled with epoxy resin filler or bituminous mastic compound. Finish with rust inhibiting primer and paint. Gutters are often painted with bituminous paint, a thick black paint that gives ideal protection.

Always remember that rust action will start again immediately in any exposed metal that has just been cleaned, so always plan to clean and prime metal in one session.

Rust can appear as a discolouration on brickwork joints, or around ironwork embedded in brickwork. The brickwork can flake and crack as a result, so rake out the mortar around the ironwork, then clean and prime the metal.

Rust in brick jointing occurs as a result of ironstone in the sand. The mortar will have to be raked out and repointed.

Rot

Dry and wet rot destroy timber. Both are caused by fungi that originate in wet timber in damp and poorly ventilated situations, such as under sinks or in cellars. The dry rot fungus differs in that it can spread from damp to dry timber. It is therefore much more serious and difficult to contain. Its ability to spread throughout a house can have a devastating effect on a building, totally destroying structural and flooring timbers.

A typical dry rot attack could start in the floor joists. Matted fungal strands develop and combine to form a silvery-grey skin. The skin can be patched or streaked with lilac or yellow, and eventually turns into a cotton-wool-like texture resembling a white cushion. The edges of the cushion sometimes turn bright yellow if exposed to light.

At this stage any affected timber will become dark brown, and cracks will develop both with and across the grain thus breaking down the surface into a covering of cubes. The wood will also buckle, and will crumble if rubbed with the fingers.

As the fungus develops, a pale grey, corrugated fruiting body resembling a pancake will form, surrounded by a covering of rusty-red spore dust.

Having destroyed the damp wood in which it originated, the fungus then seeks to create ideal living conditions on nearby timber. It does this by producing water carrying roots which can be up to 6mm (¼in) in diameter. These roots can reach anywhere, even through brickwork, until they find dry timber which they dampen to form another breeding ground for the fungus to thrive on and destroy.

As the fungus starts in normally unseen places, the first evidence of it existence may be seen as a cotton wool cushion showing from beneath floorboards or from behind skirtings or panelling on walls. In more advanced attacks, when the fruiting body has formed, a mushroom-like smell might be the first indication of its existence.

A dry, structurally sound house will not allow a dry rot attack to develop. All the precautions stipulated in the chapter on Damp and condensation (see pages 62-69) should be observed to ensure that the house remains dry and well-ventilated.

If damp has shown itself inside the house, and especially if it has been left unchecked for a long period, make a thorough check of the house, especially in cellars or under floorboards, looking closely for any of the telltale signs of dry rot.

Treatment of dry rot

The effective treatment of a dry rot attack depends on the extent of the attack and how thoroughly and efficiently the householder is prepared to check the whole building and carry out remedial treatment. As the fungus has the ability to travel long distances and through walls, areas far from the site of the original outbreak may require treatment.

An attack that has affected structural timbers will certainly require expert attention to cut out damaged timber and replace it with new material.

The search for and eradication of dry rot must be ruthless. Any affected timber must be cut out at least 1m beyond all visible evidence of attack. Where the water carrying roots have travelled through walls, plaster and mortar joints must be hacked out. An attack under a floor laid over an earth sub-site may have to be treated by digging out about 100mm (4in) of soil to expose the site of the fungus.

As soon as the entire affected area and beyond has been cleared, all debris must be removed immediately from the building and burnt. This will prevent the decay from spreading and stop the red spore dust from being carried by the wind into nearby buildings.

Dry rot treatment requires an initial spraying

RIGHT: *Removing wood damaged by wet rot from window frame.*
FAR RIGHT: *Dry rot can completely disintegrate wood structures.*

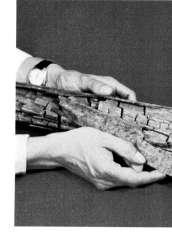

with a proprietary dry rot fungicidal fluid, using a coarse sprayer in accordance with the manufacturer's instructions. Spreading rates are usually in the order of 5 litres to 5m² (approx. 9 pints to 6sq.yd).

All walls, concrete, steel, pipework, earth and timber within a radius of 1½m (5ft) of the last suspected sign of infection must be sprayed with two coats of fluid (allowing the first to dry) and wire brushed. Any debris must be removed and burnt immediately.

Surface spores and strands on walls can be sterilised by heat from a blowlamp. The water carrying roots already in the wall can be killed by drilling 12mm (½in) diameter holes, 150mm (6in) deep at 600mm (24in) staggered centres around the infected area. Slope the holes downwards at 45 degrees. It is necessary to drill on both sides of the wall. Fill the holes with fluid and leave it to soak in and kill off the roots.

At this stage, the structural defect in the house that gave rise to the problem must be corrected.

New replacement timber must be dry and well-seasoned. Treat it with two coats of fungicidal wood preservative. Steep any sawn ends in the preservative for a few minutes before use.

Where rotting timber is cut away, all other timber within a radius of 1½m (5ft) should be given two coats of fungicidal dry rot fluid at a rate of 5 litres to 18m² (approx. 9 pints to 21sq.yd). Allow the first coat to soak in before applying the second coat.

Where walls are to be finished with a setting coat of plaster for redecorating, the first rendering coat should be a normal 1:1:6 (cement:lime:sand) mix. The second coat should be of 6mm thick zinc oxychloride plaster applied to an area to within 300mm (12in) of any affected timber. The third coat should be another normal 1:1:6 rendering mix applied to all areas adjacent to the second coat. The final coat should be a setting coat of retarded hemi-hydrate plaster.

Two coats of zinc oxychloride paint can be used instead of zinc oxychloride plaster for walls that are not to be replastered.

Treatment of wet rot

Wet rot can also be found in cellars, roofs, bathrooms and kitchens as well as in outdoor timbers of fences and sheds. It is far easier to treat, however, since it will be confined to wet timber. It cannot transfer itself to dry timber, although it must be remembered that a dry rot attack could be in progress nearby.

The wet rot fungus originates with yellowish-brown streaks or patches accompanied by stringlike strands growing in a fern shape on timber or damp plaster. The wood becomes brownish-black and cracks along the grain, although cracks across the grain causing a cuboid effect on the surface are common. In severe attacks, the wood, if rubbed, will crumble into powder.

Bubbling paintwork is often the first indication of wet rot thriving below surface. A probe with a sharp penknife may reveal crumbling wood below. The penknife should be used to establish the extent of an attack.

To cure wet rot, cut out completely rotted timber. Affected timber that can be salvaged should be given two liberal coats of dry rot fluid or wood preservative, and surrounding walls should be treated before use as described in the section on dry rot.

Paint the ends of new timber joists with bituminous paint or cover them with bituminous felt before insertion.

Areas requiring replastering should be rendered with a normal 1:1:6 rendering mix, as for dry rot treatment. Wall surfaces in the area of attack should be finished with anhydrous plaster.

BELOW LEFT: *Dry rot fungus produces these typical fruiting bodies.* BELOW: *Skirting boards can be completely distorted by an infestation of dry rot fungus.*

Woodworm

The arrival of an adult woodbeetle in your house could be followed within a few weeks by a woodworm munching its way ravenously through timber in the loft, cellar, floorboards, joists, furniture, or anywhere in the house.

The diligent householder will make an annual inspection for woodworm infestation or, preferably, prevent attacks by protecting timber in the house. The less careful owner is likely to have the problem brought to his notice when he sells the house, when a simple survey by the purchaser or a professional surveyor will reveal evidence of woodworm. Immediate treatment will be necessary, usually paid for by the householder. A building society will often refuse to hand over a complete mortgage to a purchaser until treatment has been carried out.

The extra bill, and considerable inconvenience, will occur at the least convenient time and the whole buying-and-selling transaction could be jeopardised.

It is fortunate that houses change hands and are surveyed so regularly or the estimated woodworm infestation of over half the houses in Britain might be greater.

Even if your house is clear of woodworm, it could be attacked next year; take preventative action now or take out an insurance policy to cover the cost of any future treatment.

Types of woodworm

Furniture beetle Most woodworm attacks are made by the furniture beetle. The adult beetle is about 3mm to 5mm (⅛in to ¼in) long and has a rusty-black colouring. It is usually found in damp, rotting wood but also likes dry timber. It can infest structural timbers, joinery and furniture.

The adult beetle lays its eggs on rough timbers, such as those commonly found in cellars and lofts. It will also seek out cracks and crevices in smooth-faced timber.

Egg-laying time is from May to August. On warm days during this period the beetles may be seen flying around and crawling on walls and windows. A beetle lays about 60 eggs, which hatch after a few weeks. The grubs eat their way downwards into the wood and will continue eating for about three years. Each grub eats timber at the rate of about two inches a year, forming little tunnels as it goes along. With possibly hundred of grubs at work, the timber is weakened considerably. Towards the end of their three years, the grubs head for the surface where they change first into a chrysalis and then the adult beetle, which pushes its way through the surface of the wood, leaving a hole about 1mm to 2mm (¹⁄₁₆in) in diameter, surrounded by a little pile of whitish dust.

The female beetle then searches for a mate and within a month it will have laid a crop of new eggs in timber crevices.

Powder post beetle This beetle is slightly slimmer and longer. As it emerges in its adult form it makes a similar exit hole in the wood surface, also surrounded by dust. It is most prolific in July, although it can be seen flying around any time during the summer months. It is often seen at dusk when the weather is warm and has the same colouring as the furniture beetle.

ABOVE: *The larva of the furniture beetle feeds on the timber.*
RIGHT: *The woodworm beetle bores hundreds of tiny holes in timber as shown here.*

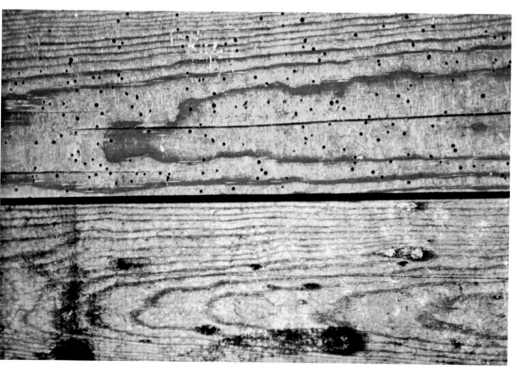

It has been given the name of powder post beetle because it can quite literally reduce timber to powder.

House longhorn beetle Confined to the south of England, this beetle is enormously destructive, and most generally attacks roof timbers. Each grub may remain in the wood for ten years before emerging and attacks may not be detected until a considerable amount of damage has been caused below surface. Blistered wood is an early indication; when the blister is burst it reveals a powdery surface underneath.

Exit holes are irregularly shaped slits and may be 9mm (⅜in) wide. The adult beetle is blackish-brown and up to 20mm (¾in) long.

Evidence of the house longhorn beetle must be reported to the Princes Risborough Laboratory of the Building Research Establishment, Princes Risborough, Bucks.

Death watch beetle This one is likely to affect only a very old house with oak beams, particularly if the house is dampish and rarely heated. The adult beetle is dark brown and about 6mm (¼in) long. The exit hole it makes in the timber is 3mm (⅛in) in diameter. It is famous for the tapping sound it makes to attract a mate, which it does by knocking its head against wood. It is sometimes heard in old churches from April to June.

Woodboring weevil Huge infestations of this common beetle may occur, but only in rotten timber. It usually tunnels along the grain of the timber, leaving a pin-prick size hole when the grub emerges. The adult beetle is about 5mm (³/₁₆in) long.

Checking timber for woodworm attack

The best time to inspect timber for woodworm attack is in the early summer when the grubs have recently emerged and the adults are flying around. The tell-tale holes are usually found on horizontal surfaces and will be surrounded by dust. Holes without dust generally indicate an attack that has died off or has been killed off by past woodworm treatment.

The best starting point for an inspection is the loft, which is notorious for established attacks, as many lofts are visited briefly only a few times each year. If the loft is insulated (which it should be) the sides of the joists will be hidden from view by the insulating material.

Check under the floorboards in the rest of the house. These are rarely seen once a fitted floorcovering has been laid and years could pass before an established woodworm attack is spotted. A thorough inspection requires lifting sufficient boards to see below them and to check the joists.

Check the cellar, skirtings, cupboards, wall panelling, especially plywood, and furniture, especially any recently acquired second hand items.

Treating woodworm

Preparing surfaces for treatment If an attack is spotted, especially in the loft, wear your working clothes to clean the area before treatment.

Lofts are often cluttered up and it is best to plan the treatment in two stages. Stored goods will have to be piled in one corner and covered while the remaining area is dusted and sprayed. The goods can be moved to the treated area while the second area is cleaned and sprayed.

If the cold water storage cistern is uncovered, make sure it is well protected during cleaning and spraying. (Make a note to construct a permanent cover for the cistern; dust, insects and dead birds are not desirable in water for use in the bathroom.)

Cisterns that have been insulated with expanded polystyrene sheets will have to be covered before using the spray and so will any rubber covered cables, as the insecticide will damage both materials. A coat of wood sealer will protect cables.

When everything is out of the way, the timbers can be brushed and vacuum cleaned and all the dust collected in polythene sacks.

Applying woodworm fluid in the loft Woodworm fluid is sold by builders' merchants under various brand names. Usual application rate for the fluid is about 1 litre to 4m² (approx. 2 pints to 5sq.yd) of timber area. To calculate the required amount, measure the surface area of all timbers to be treated. This can be done quickly for joists by estimating the surface of one joist and multiplying the result by the number of joists in the loft.

Woodworm fluid is often sold in 25 litre (44 pint) drums and the average house roof will require two drums. Check manufacturer's application rates and other instructions before use.

A pneumatic garden sprayer is needed to apply the fluid. This should hold about five litres and produce a moderately coarse spray. If the nozzle of the spray is too coarse, excessive fluid will be used and much of it will simply run off the timbers; if the nozzle is too fine, the spray will not be sufficiently powerful to penetrate the timber.

Certain safety rules must be strictly adhered to when using woodworm fluid. You must wear a light fume mask and goggles, and protect any exposed skin by rubbing in barrier cream. Wear leather gloves, as rubber perishes when the fluid drops on it. Observe a strict no smoking rule in the area during spraying and for at least 24 hours afterwards. If you need a torch, the recommended type is a portable flameproof handlamp connected to a socket outlet outside the treatment area.

Spray all surfaces in the loft. Give any cracks, crevices and end grain a thorough soaking.

ABOVE: *Most woodworm attacks are by the furniture beetle.*

ABOVE: *The powder post beetle is a common woodworm species.*

ABOVE: *The house longhorn beetle attacks roof timbers.*

ABOVE: *The death watch beetle is usually found in older houses.*

ABOVE: *The woodboring weevil only attacks rotten timber.*

Though floor joists will have to be treated, any ceiling laths will usually be covered well enough by fall-out from the spray.

Never delay the treatment of a woodworm attack. Treatment can be carried out at any time of the year. If the spray is applied correctly and the fluid seeps into the timber, any grubs already below surface will be poisoned as they eat their way out. There will be some odour left after treatment but this will dissipate quickly as the fluid dries in. Any temporarily removed insulation material can be reinstated and the loft returned to its normal state.

Treating woodworm elsewhere in the house
The same treatment can be used for all other areas in the house and application rate and the coarseness of the spray nozzle are the same.

To be totally effective, treatment must be painstakingly thorough. Floorboards will have to be raised at regular intervals to spray their undersides and the joists below, using an extension lance fitted to the sprayer. The ends of joists where they enter a wall cannot be sprayed and are treated with deep penetration paste, which is spread on the surface of the timber and left to soak in.

The floorcovering can be relaid after a week. If this has to be done after only two days, a sheet of polythene can first be laid over the floorboards.

If skirtings or panelling are only slightly affected by woodworm, surface treatment should be sufficient. Where an attack is severe, however, the timber will have to be removed to treat any studding timbers behind.

Special woodworm injector aerosols are used for treating furniture. These have pointed nozzles designed to fit into the woodworm holes. It is sufficient to inject the fluid into holes every three or four inches, or according to manufacturer's instructions. Treat drawers, inside the carcase, and the undersides of the feet. Unpolished surfaces should receive a further spray treatment. Give any end grain, joints and so on, a thorough soaking.

The furniture will not require future treatments. An occasional application of woodworm polish to all parts, polished and unpolished, will prevent woodworm.

Do not attempt to treat upholstered furniture or any valuable items. These should be handled only by experts.

Never attempt to deal with a really severe woodworm attack. In such cases, it is better to seek the help of a reputable specialist company, who generally guarantee the treatment for 20 or more years.

Continue to check any treated areas for a year. Thorough treatment kills the woodworm and there will be no further signs. However if the attack persists, repeat the treatment at the time of year when the beetles emerge from their flight holes.

Household pests

Most insects that enter the house can be killed with one of the many widely available insecticides. Rodents, too, can be killed with proprietary baits.

Persistent or extensive attacks, especially by cockroaches and rodents, need immediate expert handling and local authority health departments or specialist companies (see Yellow Pages) should be called in.

Identification and treatment of common pests

Ants The black garden ant enters the house in search of sweet foodstuffs to take back to the nest for the queen and larvae.
CURE: If garden nests can be treated, pour in boiling water and puff insecticidal powder into the nest. Alternatively, spread insecticidal lacquer around door thresholds and ant runs.

Liquid or jelly baits placed on runs are taken back to the nest and poison the queen and larvae.

Carpet beetle This insect feeds on fur, feathers and wool, and resembles a ladybird but has a mottled grey, brown and cream coat. It is 2 to 4mm (1/8in) long, and is related to the fur beetle, which is black with a white spot on each wing. They often find their way into an airing cupboard and settle in sheets and linen from where they can be spread throughout the house.
CURE: Clear dead birds or nests from lofts. Vacuum-clean dust and fluff from cupboards, shelves, carpets, underfelt, upholstery. Spray with carpet beetle killer or proprietary moth-proofer. Dust insect powder around previously vacuumed areas.

Cockroaches Rarely found in the house. They hide by day near warm pipes, stoves and sinks, emerging at night for food. They carry various diseases and cause serious food poisoning.
CURE: Clean all food residues from storage areas. Puff insect powder into crevices and other likely hiding places. Inaccessible hiding places are difficult to treat. Persistent attacks need expert handling, and should be notified to your local health authority.

Earwigs A harmless intruder that usually enters on cut flowers.
CURE: Cut wallclimbing plants well back from doors and windows. Dust corners where earwigs congregate with insecticidal powder.

Flies Cause food poisoning and diseases.
CURE: Dispose of all refuse quickly. Keep all food in sealed containers. Spray inside the house with insecticide. Impregnated plastic strips or containers which emit a slow-killing vapour should be hung away from children, work-

surfaces or food. Fly screens can be fitted to open windows.

Mice Field mice and house mice enter houses for food and warmth. They damage stored food, nibble woodwork, electric cables and water pipes. Mice are a source of serious food poisoning and other diseases.

CURE: Block all likely entry points to the house. Use a rodenticide for mice.

Traditional traps will catch the occasional mouse, if baited with raisins, chocolate or similar foods.

A persistent or serious outbreak needs expert help.

Moths The two common types are the brown house moth and the white shouldered house moth. Their grubs feed on woollen fabrics especially and cause the familiar damage. Clothes stained with perspiration or urine are more susceptible to attack.

CURE: Man-made fibres are immune to attack. Clean all woollens before storing them in drawers or cupboards. Wrap them in tightly sealed polythene bags or paper bags and slip a moth repellent disc inside the bag. Hang Mothaks or moth-proofer strips in wardrobes. Clean edges of upholstery and carpets. Spray attacked items with mothproofer, especially folds and seams.

Rats The brown rat is about 225mm (9in) long and weighs about half a kilo (1lb). The black rat is slightly shorter and half as heavy. Both types spread serious diseases and cause food poisoning. They nibble and damage woodwork, electric cables and water pipes.

CURE: Poison rats with a proprietary bait, taking care to follow the manufacturer's instructions. It is supplied in sachets and should be placed where rats run, usually along skirtings and fences. Replace the baits until no more are taken. Food put out for the birds should be placed on a bird table.

Any persistent or extensive rat attack must be dealt with immediately by experts.

Silverfish Grey insects about 12mm (½in) long. They inhabit damp areas in bathrooms and kitchens and are sometimes seen in the bottom of bread bins. They feed on starchy substances such as carbohydrate food deposits and wallpaper paste. They usually emerge only at night.

CURE: Cure any dampness. Fill cracks in floors and skirtings. Spray with insecticide or powder.

Spiders Harmless, more of a nuisance.

CURE: Spray directly or into hiding places with insecticide.

Wasps Enter in search of sweet foodstuffs.

CURE: Put fly screen over open windows. Keep all food covered. Remove waste immediately and clean all surfaces. Spray directly on to wasps with wasp killer. Use these sprays very carefully, especially indoors.

LEFT: *The carpet beetle looks like a ladybird. It can do great damage to woollen carpets.*
BELOW LEFT: *Earwigs are quite harmless, and do no damage in the household.*
BELOW: *Cockroaches are nocturnal, and are therefore hard to spot. They can carry various diseases, including food poisoning.*

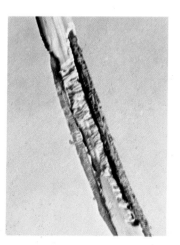

LEFT: *The brown house moth attacks natural fibres like woollen fabrics.*
BELOW LEFT: *Rats have nibbled right through the casing of this electric cable.*
BELOW: *More rat damage, this time to a piece of lead pipe.*

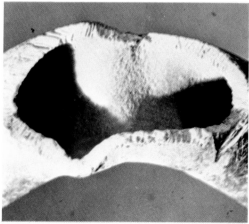

77

Ready reference

Tool kit

General household repair and maintenance jobs require many tools. For instance, the relatively simple job of replacing window glass calls for a screwdriver or chisel to clear out the old putty, and pincers or pliers to pull out the sprigs or nails holding the glass. A steel tape is needed for measuring up the new pane, and a paint brush for priming the frame. A small hammer will be required for tapping the glass securing sprigs into place, and for a smooth finish a putty knife is essential.

The best way to assemble a took kit is to buy the basic tools, which are described below, and add to them when necessary. Always buy the best tools you can afford, as these should last a lifetime and will give first class results.

It is possible to hire most tools on a daily or weekly basis. The address of a local hire shop will be found in Yellow Pages under Hire Contractors.

Basic tool kit

A 3m/10ft **dual-marked steel measuring tape** (1) will cover most measuring jobs. Buy one with a lock to hold the tape in the out position while in use. Some types have a window in the top of the case to allow easy measurements of internal recesses.

One of the most basic home repair jobs is drilling holes. For manual operation, you can use the **hand drill** (2) (for holes up to about 6mm/½in).

A **set of small twist drills** (3) in sizes from 1.5mm to 7mm (¹/₁₆in to ¼in is the nearest equivalent) will be required. For drilling walls you will need a special **tungsten carbide tipped masonry drill** (4). A good size is 6.5mm (¼in) which will take many plastic wallplugs suitable for gauge 6, 8, and 10 screws. For bigger holes you can use the brace (5), for which you will need **a set of auger bits** (6).

An ordinary **single slot screwdriver** (7) about 8mm (⁵/₁₆in) across the blade will be adequate for most purposes. For cross head Pozidriver or Superdriv screws a **screwdriver with a matching head** (8) will be required. There are three head sizes. The most useful size is No. 2 point which drives gauge 5 to 10 Superdriv screws.

For electrical work buy a **mains tester screwdriver** (9) which has a narrow blade to fit terminal screws in plugs and sockets, an insulated shank, and a neon in the handle for checking circuits are dead before work starts.

A 570g (20oz) **claw hammer** (10) is suitable for general nailing. The claw is used for extracting nails.

Smaller nails and pins can be fixed with a 225g (8oz) **Warrington or cross pein hammer** (11). One side of the hammer is of conventional shape and the other is wedge-shaped. Either side can be used for nailing, depending on the size of nail and space available.

For extracting nails and tacks where a claw hammer cannot be used, a pair of 180mm (7in) **pincers** (12) is useful. For general gripping and for cutting wire, electric cable, and flex use a pair of 150mm (6in) **electrician's pliers** (13).

A multitude of trimming and cutting work can be carried out with a **multi-blade trimming knife** (14). Choose one with a handle that fits comfortably in the palm of your hand.

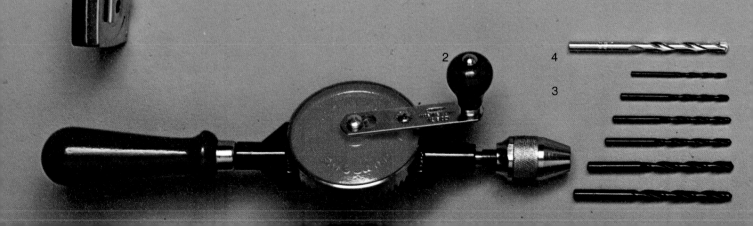

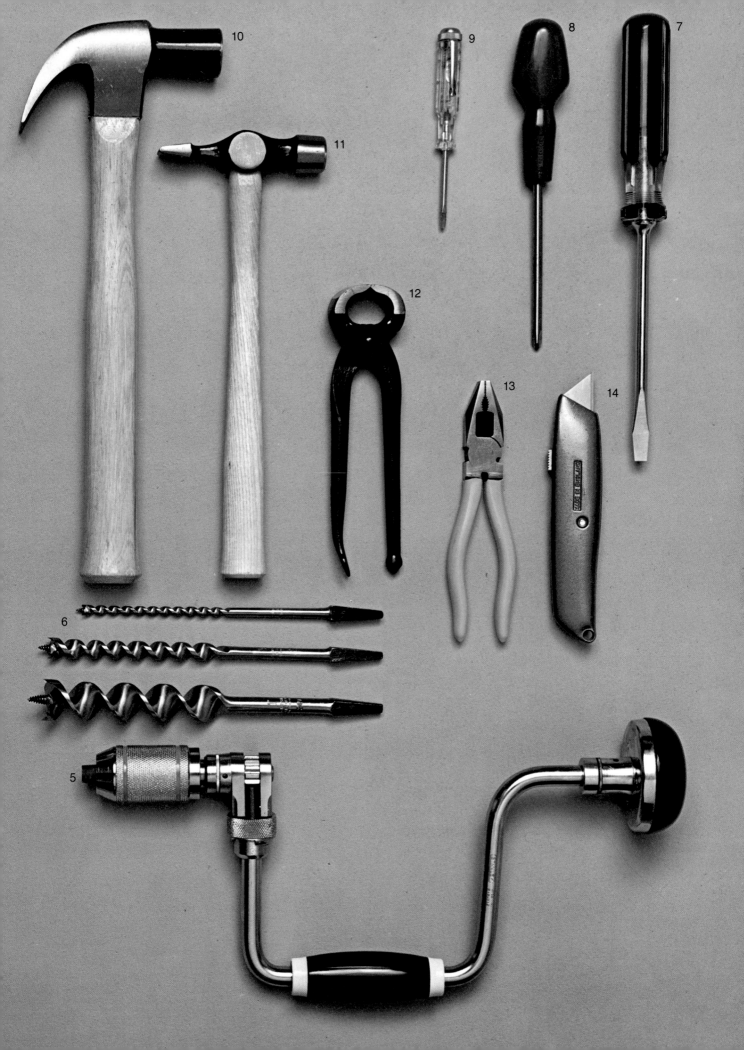

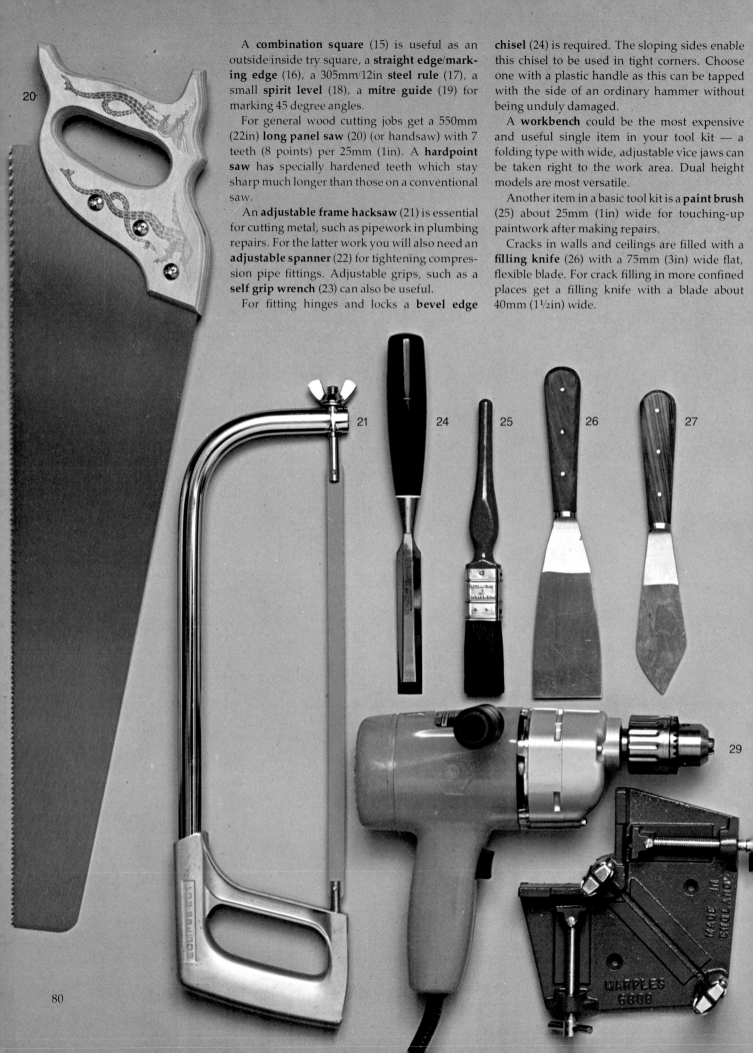

A **combination square** (15) is useful as an outside/inside try square, a **straight edge/marking edge** (16), a 305mm/12in **steel rule** (17), a small **spirit level** (18), a **mitre guide** (19) for marking 45 degree angles.

For general wood cutting jobs get a 550mm (22in) **long panel saw** (20) (or handsaw) with 7 teeth (8 points) per 25mm (1in). A **hardpoint saw** has specially hardened teeth which stay sharp much longer than those on a conventional saw.

An **adjustable frame hacksaw** (21) is essential for cutting metal, such as pipework in plumbing repairs. For the latter work you will also need an **adjustable spanner** (22) for tightening compression pipe fittings. Adjustable grips, such as a **self grip wrench** (23) can also be useful.

For fitting hinges and locks a **bevel edge** chisel (24) is required. The sloping sides enable this chisel to be used in tight corners. Choose one with a plastic handle as this can be tapped with the side of an ordinary hammer without being unduly damaged.

A **workbench** could be the most expensive and useful single item in your tool kit — a folding type with wide, adjustable vice jaws can be taken right to the work area. Dual height models are most versatile.

Another item in a basic tool kit is a **paint brush** (25) about 25mm (1in) wide for touching-up paintwork after making repairs.

Cracks in walls and ceilings are filled with a **filling knife** (26) with a 75mm (3in) wide flat, flexible blade. For crack filling in more confined places get a filling knife with a blade about 40mm (1½in) wide.

A **putty knife** (27) with a blade about 115mm (4½in) long and curved on one side will be needed for glazing repairs.

Do not forget to keep a good **torch** (28) handy in your tool kit.

Of course, many of these hand tools can be left out of your kit if you decide to go in for power tools and attachments. A **power drill** (29) takes the effort out of drilling, and can be fitted with accessories to sand, saw and perform other jobs.

The best type is a two-speed drill with acceleration trigger control, a 10mm (⅜in) capacity chuck and hammer action. The trigger control enables speeds to be adjusted for drilling in different materials, such as wood, metal and brick. Generally, the harder the material and the bigger the hole, the slower the speed of the drill. Hammer action can be selected.

Other basic materials

As well as a basic and an emergency tool kit, it is advisable to have a basic stock of certain materials which might be required urgently.

Tap washers — 13mm (½in) (sink/basin) and 20mm (¾in) (bath)

Full Stop set — 13mm and 20mm (½in and ¾in) (if tap seating is worn)

Washer plate/jumpers for Supataps (the type where the outlet spout hangs down and is movable)

O-ring seals (to stop head leaks in shrouded-head taps)

Washers for ball valves in cisterns (to mend overflows)

Rubber diaphragms for modern ball valves

Spare lavatory cistern flap valves

Card of fuse wire (for fuses in the consumer unit) or cartridge fuses (if this type of fuse carrier is fitted)

3amp and 13amp cartridge fuses for plugs

Terminal connector strips (to join cable or flex if necessary)

Plastic adhesive tape

Plastic green/yellow coloured earth sleeving for use on un-insulated earth wires

Epoxy resin adhesive

Cyanoacrylate adhesive

Glass fibre repair kit

Waterproof mastic tape

Selection of wood screws, wall plugs, and cavity wall fixings

Asbestos compound screw-fixing filler.

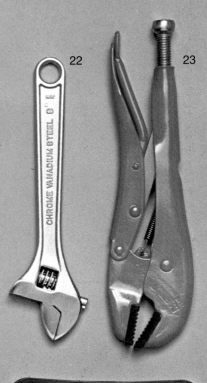

Adhesives

There are hundreds of adhesives on the market to cope with almost every job, but a few well-chosen ones will cover most situations. For example, **(Opposite)** a pva adhesive is excellent for woodwork, while high strength epoxy resins are ideal for small-scale, high-strength jobs.

Adhesives have undergone tremendous advances in recent years and there is now a strong, clean and quick-setting adhesive for most materials.

In all cases it is important to read the instructions carefully and follow them to the letter. Take particular care over surface preparation. The surfaces to be joined must be snug-fitting, dry and free from grease and dust.

Exercise caution when using adhesives. Use adhesives in a well-ventilated area and avoid inhaling the fumes as some release chemicals which can damage the lining of the nose and throat. Always keep adhesives in a cool place away from children. The quicksetting cyano-acrylates in particular must be kept away from eyes and skin, although this precaution should be observed with all types of adhesives.

Different types of adhesives

Animal glues Some types are supplied in solid bars or beads which must be heated for use. Other types are supplied in slow-drying liquid form. They are used mainly for fixing wood veneers, but have been largely superseded for most jobs by pva glues. Used on wood, cardboard, china, paper and leather.
SOLVENT — water

Contact adhesives Applied to both parts and allowed to become touch-dry before surfaces are brought together. Not suitable for highly stressed wood-to-wood joints. Most types are highly flammable except the water-based versions.

Use to bond wood, rigid pvc, plastic laminates, metal, rubber, plasterboard, smooth concrete, leather, canvas. Water-based types will stick expanded polystyrene.
SOLVENT — acetone, nail varnish remover and water (while still liquid) in case of water-based types.

Cyanoacrylates Stick most non-absorbent materials in seconds. Will also bond skin, so keep it away from fingers, mouth and eyes. Surfaces to be joined must be close-fitting, smooth and clean. Good for bonding metals, most plastics, rubber, hardwoods, china. Do not use to bond glass. Not waterproof. Expensive, so use for small high-strength repairs.
SOLVENT — acetone, nail varnish remover.

Epoxy resins Supplied in two parts, adhesive and hardener, which are mixed together just before use. Made in fast and slow setting types. Resists boiling water, acids, oil, heat. Will join most materials, but is expensive so it is used for small jobs where strength is required. Particularly useful for glass, china and jewellery repairs.
SOLVENT — methylated spirit while still liquid.

Glass bonding adhesives Specially developed to give a strong bond on glass or glass to metal.

Gives a clear, invisible repair which bonds in ten to 20 seconds in bright sunlight. Curing is activated by ultraviolet light in daytime but not by artificial light. In dull or cloudy weather bonding may take one to two minutes. Bond strength develops over 24 hours. Water and detergent resistant. Not suitable for oven glassware. Some coloured glasses can filter out the ultra-violet light and affect bonding.
SOLVENT — methylated spirits or acetone before curing takes place.

Gums and pastes Made from vegetable, animal and rubber derivatives. Available in powder and liquid forms and used mainly to stick wallpaper, cardboard, paper, leather and expanded polystyrene wall veneers.
SOLVENT — water.

Household adhesives Transparent, quick-drying and moderately waterproof. Many have a cellulose base and are used for general purpose repairs to most household materials except expanded polystyrene or polythene.
SOLVENT — acetone or nail varnish remover.

Latex adhesives Creamy, white adhesives which dry clear and give a strong flexible bond on carpets, fabrics and cardboard. Resists water.
SOLVENT — lighter fuel.

Mastics Various types. Used as outdoor flooring, tiling, board and wall panel adhesives. Some are applied to only one surface, others to both. Some are applied with a notched spreader, others with a mastic gun. Good for gap filling where surfaces to be joined do not meet exactly, that is, when sticking plasterboard to a brick or block wall. Water resistant.
SOLVENT — petrol, paraffin.

Polyvinyl acetate (pva) Supplied as a ready-to-use white liquid. Dries clear. Non-toxic. Gives a strong bond, but has poor water resistance. Used mainly for woodworking joints, but will also bond paper, fabrics, card, leather.

Pva-base adhesive pastes applied with a notched spreader are used to fix ceramic and expanded polystyrene tiles to walls and ceilings.
SOLVENT — water.

Plastic cements Used on rigid polystyrene products. Fuses the plastics. Dries fast and clear. Moisture resistant. Not suitable for expanded or foam polystyrene.
SOLVENT — acetone or nail varnish remover — solvents will damage the plastic.

Polyvinyl chloride (pvc) Used for sticking flexible pvc plastics and vinyls. Gives strong, flexible fused join. Not suitable for polythene, which is joined by heat welding or with self-adhesive tape.
SOLVENT — acetone or nail varnish remover — solvents will damage the pvc.

Synthetic resins Two types. **Resorcinol formaldehydes** are two-part adhesives which are mixed together and form a strong, highly water resistant adhesive for wood. Excellent for boat building and outdoor furniture.

Urea formaldehydes are usually a powder of adhesive with hardener which is mixed with water to form a creamy paste. Strong, water resistant, gap-filling adhesive for wood. Use indoors or out.

Another form has adhesive which is applied to one surface and hardener which is applied to the other. Setting begins when the surfaces are joined.
SOLVENT — warm water while liquid.

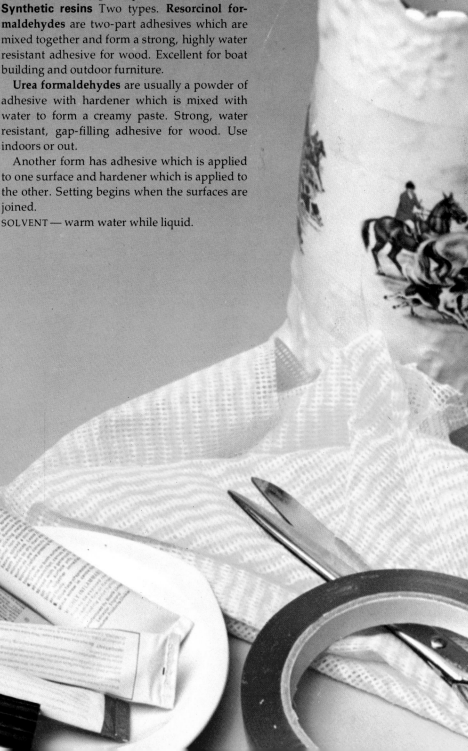

Metrication

The changeover to the International Metric System has affected many aspects of home repairs.

Metrication has been implemented fully in the building trade and timber, sand and cement, bricks, paint, plumbing fittings and electric cable are now sold in metric units.

In many other areas, some products are available in both metric and imperial sizes. This applies to ceramic floor and wall tiles, and to concrete paving slabs. Unfortunately the metric and imperial sizes do not match exactly and it is almost impossible to use a successful combination of the two sizes.

This problem is exemplified by 6 × 6in. wall tiles, which measure 152 × 152mm. The nearest equivalent metric tiles are 150 × 150mm, slightly under 6in. square. It is essential to work in metric or imperial units throughout a job.

Timber As this is fully metricated, measure and work in metric units. Sawn softwood is available in a standard range of lengths beginning at 1.8m (5ft 10⅞in) and increasing in steps of 300mm (11 ¹³/₁₆in) to 6.3m (20ft 8in). Retailers will usually supply shorter and longer pieces.

Standard widths and thicknesses of sawn softwood are shown on page 86. Small sections are re-sawn from standard sections to give the following sizes:- 25 × 25mm, 25 × 38mm, 25 × 50mm and 50 × 50mm.

Boards Plywood, blockboard, hardboard, insulation board and plasterboard are sold in metric lengths, widths and thicknesses which are close to the old imperial sizes. The popular 8 × 4ft sheet is sold as 2440 × 1220mm. Fully metric sheets such as 2400 × 1200mm (about 7ft 10½in × 3ft 11¼in) are being introduced.

Bricks There is now a standard metric brick which is slightly smaller than the imperial one. The new brick can be used with existing brickwork if the mortar joints are increased slightly (see page 86).

Concrete building blocks These are available in a range of 16 coordinated metric sizes. The most popular sizes (including the mortar joint) are 400 × 100mm, 400 × 200mm, 450 × 200mm, 450 × 225mm, and 450 × 300mm. These blocks match with standard metric bricks (see page 86).

Concrete blocks measuring 448 × 219mm (18 × 9in including the mortar joint) and 397 × 194mm (16 × 8in including the mortar joint) are available for maintenance and repair work.

Paint This is sold in metric size cans. Page 86 shows the approximate spreading capacity of each size. Brushes are still in imperial widths, but they fit into the new tins.

Plumbing Metal pipes and fittings are sold in metric sizes. Metric copper pipe is measured externally, although other types are still measured conventionally by their inside diameter. The new sizes are shown on page 87.

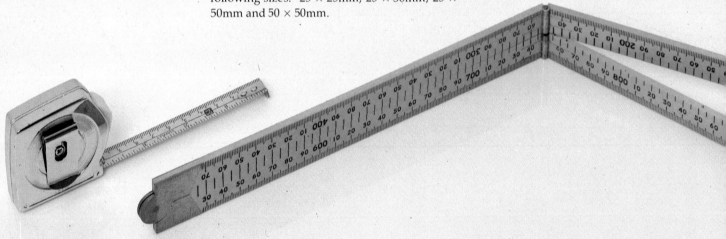

These sizes are nominal and planed timber will always measure less than sawn sizes.

Sawn hardwood is available in a standard range of lengths beginning at 1.8m and increasing in steps of 100mm (3¹⁵/₁₆in). Shorter lengths are usually available. Standard thicknesses are 19, 25, 32, 38, 50, 63, 75 and 100mm. Widths are normally 50mm and up in steps of 10mm. Additional widths of 63, 75 and 125mm are available.

Metric compression pipe fittings are interchangeable with imperial pipe and fittings in some sizes, but require adaptors in others, (see page 87). Keep this in mind when you are making repairs or additions to any existing systems.

Metric capillary (soldered) fittings are not directly interchangeable with imperial sizes, but adaptors are available. Check at your hardware shop, and ask for the most suitable kind.

Pipe fittings which use screwed (BSP) threads to make the joint remain unchanged. Screwed fittings are used for tap, waste outlet, boiler connections and radiator connections, and for joining iron pipe in gas installations.

Fasteners The general purpose of imperial BA, BSW, BSF, UNC, and UNF bolts, screws and nuts are being replaced by the ISO Metric Coarse Thread Series. The imperial sizes are still available.

Wire nails are fully metric in length and diameter, and are sold in metric weights.

Wood screws and self-tapping screws are still made in imperial lengths and thicknesses (gauges), now sold in boxes of 100 and 200 screws, and no longer in units of a dozen.

Wallpaper Finished wallpaper has been available in nominal lengths of 10.05m (about 33ft) and in nominal widths of 530mm (about 21in) for many years.

Electric cables These are fully metricated. Cable sizes for fixed installations and flexible cords are given on page 86.

Glass Sold according to thickness which is specified in millimetres: 2mm replaces 1oz glass; 3mm — 24oz; 4mm — 32oz; and 6mm replaces ¼in plate glass. Length and width should be specified in metric units although most glass merchants will cut glass to imperial dimensions.

Sand-gravel and ready-mixed concrete Sold by the cubic metre (about 1.3cu. yd).

Cement, plaster and dry mortar mixes Sold in metric quantities, usually 5, 25 and 50kg bags. 50kg is just over 1cwt (110.23lb).

Metric note

				Symbol
Mega	means	×	1000000	M
Kilo	means	×	1000	K
Hecto	means	×	100	h
Deca	means	×	10	da
Deci	means	÷	10	d
Centi	means	÷	100	c
Milli	means	÷	1000	m
Micro	means	÷	1000000	μ

Length

Imperial	Metric	Metric	Imperial
1 inch	25·4mm	1mm	0·039in
1 foot	305mm	10mm (1cm)	0·394in
1 yard	0·914 metre	1 metre	1·094yd
1 mile	1·609km	1km	0·6214 mile

Approximate guide:
4in = 100mm
11yd = 10 metres
6 miles = 10 kilometres

Area

Imperial	Metric	Metric	Imperial
1sq ft (ft²)	0·093m²	1m²	10·76ft²
1sq yd (yd²)	0·836m²	1m²	1·196yd²
1 acre (4840yd²)	4046·86m²	1 hectare (10000m²)	2·4711 acres

Approximate guide: 12yd² = 10m²

Weight

Imperial	Metric	Metric	Imperial
1 lb	0·4536kg	1kg (1000g)	2·2046lb
1 ton	1·0161 tonnes	1 tonne (1000kg)	0·9842 ton

Capacity

Imperial	Metric	Metric	Imperial
1cu yd³	0·7646m³	1m³	1·308yd³

Approximate guide: 4yd³ = 3m³

Temperature

Fahrenheit to Celsius (Centigrade)	Celsius to Fahrenheit
$C = F - 32 \times \frac{5}{9}$	$F = C \times \frac{9}{5} + 32$

Approximate guide:

Fahrenheit	32	40	50	60	65	70	75	80
Celsius	0	4·5	10	15·5	18	21	24	26·6

Approximately:
A difference of 10°F = difference of 5·5°C

Bricks

The format of the standard metric brick, including the mortar joint, is 225 × 112·5 × 75 millimetres. The work size is 215 × 102·5 × 65mm. *Work size* is the size of the brick itself and is subject to tolerance.

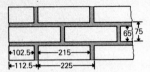

Dimensions in millimetres

Comparison of metric/imperial brick format

	Metric		Imperial	
	mm	(in)	in	(mm)
Length (including joint)	225	(8·86)	9	(228·6)
Width (incl. joint)	112·5	(4·43)	4½	(114·3)
Height (incl. joint)	75	(2·95)	3	(76·2)
Typical joint	10	(0·39)	⅜	(9·5)

Concrete building blocks

Concrete building blocks are often used with bricks – for example to form the inner leaf of cavity walling. This is how metric building blocks may be used with the standard metric brick.

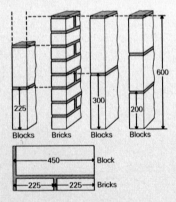

Dimensions in millimetres

Paint coverage

Approximate spreading capacity in square metres on non-porous surfaces

Metric tin sizes	Primer	Gloss	Emulsion
5 litres	60	75	90
2·5 litres	30	37	45
1 litre	12	15	18
500ml	6	7½	9
250ml	3	3½	4½

1 square metre is approximately 1.20 square yards.

Cable sizes for fixed installations
(pvc twin and earth sheathed)

New cable (mm²)	Old cable	Current rating in amps (max.)	Circuit fuse	Use
1	1/·044	12	5	Lighting
1·5	3/·029	15	15	Lighting
2·5	7/·029	21	30 (ring)	Immersion heater, ring circuit and spurs, radial circuit on 20 amp fuse
4	7/·036	28	30*	Radial circuit on 30 amp fuse
6	7/·044	35	45*	Cooker

*Cartridge fuse permits current rating of these cables to be uprated by 1/3rd, subject to voltage drop depending on length of circuit cable run.

Flexible cord ratings

New mm²	Old equivalent	No. and dia. (mm) of wires	Rating (amps)	Use
0·5	14/·0076	16/·20	3	Up to 720 watts
0·75	23/·0076	24/·20	6	Up to 1·4kW
1	—	32/·20	10	Up to 2·4kW
1·5	40/·0076 (about, but 13 amps)	30/·25	15	Up to 3·6kW
2·5	70/·0076 nearest	50/·25	20	Up to 4·8kW
4	110/·0076 nearest	56/·30	25	Up to 6kW
Pvc parallel twin non-sheathed				
0·5	14/·0076	28/·15	3	Up to 700W (lights)

Basic sizes of sawn softwood

	Width in mm									
	75	100	115	125	150	175	200	225	250	300
16	o	o		o	o					
19	o	o		o	o					
22	o	o		o	o					
25	o	o		o	o	o	o	o	o	o
32	o	o	o	o	o	o	o	o	o	o
40	o	o		o	o	o	o	o	o	o
45	o	o	o	o	o	o	o	o	o	o
50	o	o	o	o	o	o	o	o	o	o
63	o			o	o	o	o	o		
75	o			o	o	o	o	o	o	
100	o				o		o		o	o
150					o		o			o
200							o			
250							o			
300										o
Thickness										

Basic lengths of sawn softwood

Length in metres

1·80	2·10	2·40	2·70	3·00	3·30	3·60	3·90
4·20	4·50	4·80	5·10	5·40	5·70	6·00	6·30

Sheet glass

Imperial	Metric
18oz is equivalent to	2mm
24oz is equivalent to	3mm
32oz is equivalent to	4mm
³/₁₆in. is equivalent to	5mm
⁷/₃₂in. is equivalent to	5·5mm
¼in. is equivalent to	6mm

Using metric compression fittings

Interchangeable sizes

mm	in
12	⅜
15	½
28	1
54	2

Sizes requiring adaptors

mm	in
22	¾
35	1¼
42	1½

Metal pipes

Fractional and metric pipe sizes

	Iron/ Steel	Copper	Lead
Nominal fractional sizes	Nominal inside diameter	Outside diameter	Inside diameter
	mm	mm	mm
3/8	10	12	10
1/2	15	15	12
3/4	20	22	20
1	25	28	25
1 1/4	32	35	32
1 1/2	40	42	40
2	50	54	50

Note: Metric copper pipe is measured externally.

Heating

The engineering industry is the last major one to change to metric, and imperial measurements may run parallel with metric until 1985. Both imperial and metric terms may be encountered as table below.

Pressure	Imperial unit	Metric unit
	inches water gauge (in wg) lb per square inch (lb/in²)	millibar (mbar) bar (bar)

$1 N/m^2$ (newtons per square metre) $= 0.000\ 145\ 038$ lbf/in² /lb force per sq in)
$1\ bar = 14.503\ 8$ lbf/in²
(One bar equals 100000 newtons per square metre)

Standard reference conditions for gas volumes

Temp.	60° Fahrenheit (60°F)	15° Celsius (15°C)
Pressure	30 inches of mercury (30″ Hg)	1013·25mbar
Sales unit	Therm	one hundred megajoules (100MJ)
Calorific value	British Thermal Units per ft³ (Btu/cu ft)	megajoules per cubic metre (MJ/m³)
Heat rate	British Thermal Units per hour (Btu/h)	kilowatt (kW) OR, where information is needed to work out running costs, use megajoules per hour in addition to kilowatts – e.g. kW(MJ±)

One kW is about 3500Btu. To obtain the kilowatt equivalent in Btu/h, multiply kW by 3412 (exact equivalent). Thus, 4000Btu equals 1·2kW (1200 watts) and 100000Btu is equivalent to 29·3kW. A therm equals 100000Btu.

Heating and plumbing

Some, but not all metric plumbing sizes are compatible with imperial. Tubes of ¼in, ½in and 1in bore are interchangeable with the metric sizes 6mm, 15mm and 28mm. Tubes of ⅜in and ¾in bore are not compatible with the 10mm and 22mm metric sizes and a reducing set or adaptor has to be used.

Safety

It is all too easy to rush into a repair job and come to grief through failing to observe basic safety rules. The first rule is to spend a few moments before tackling any repair to consider personal and general safety.

Clothing

Never wear loose clothes, particularly neckties which may be caught by power tools. Tie back long hair. Wear tough shoes with non-slip soles.

Wear rubber gloves when handling chemicals such as paint strippers. Wear thick leather gloves when handling woodworm fluids, breaking glass out of a window frame, moving rough objects such as paving slabs, or when using a blowlamp or welding equipment.

Wear plastic non-shatter spectacles when doing any job which could yield loose particles, such as wire brushing, power sanding, grinding, using a cold chisel on masonry, removing broken window glass, or drilling masonry pins which could shatter. Wear safety spectacles when using chemicals like paint strippers.

Wear a simple dust mask (a few pence from larger chemists) when carrying out dusty jobs such as sanding. This is particularly important when working in a confined area or with asbestos.

Working at a height

The use of ladders and steps creates obvious hazards, and the following precautions should be observed.

Make sure that equipment is sound, with no cracks, rotting parts, woodworm or loose joints.

BELOW: *Never take risks with your personal safety, and wear the appropriate protection for the job. Shown here are safety goggles, protective gloves and a dust mask.*

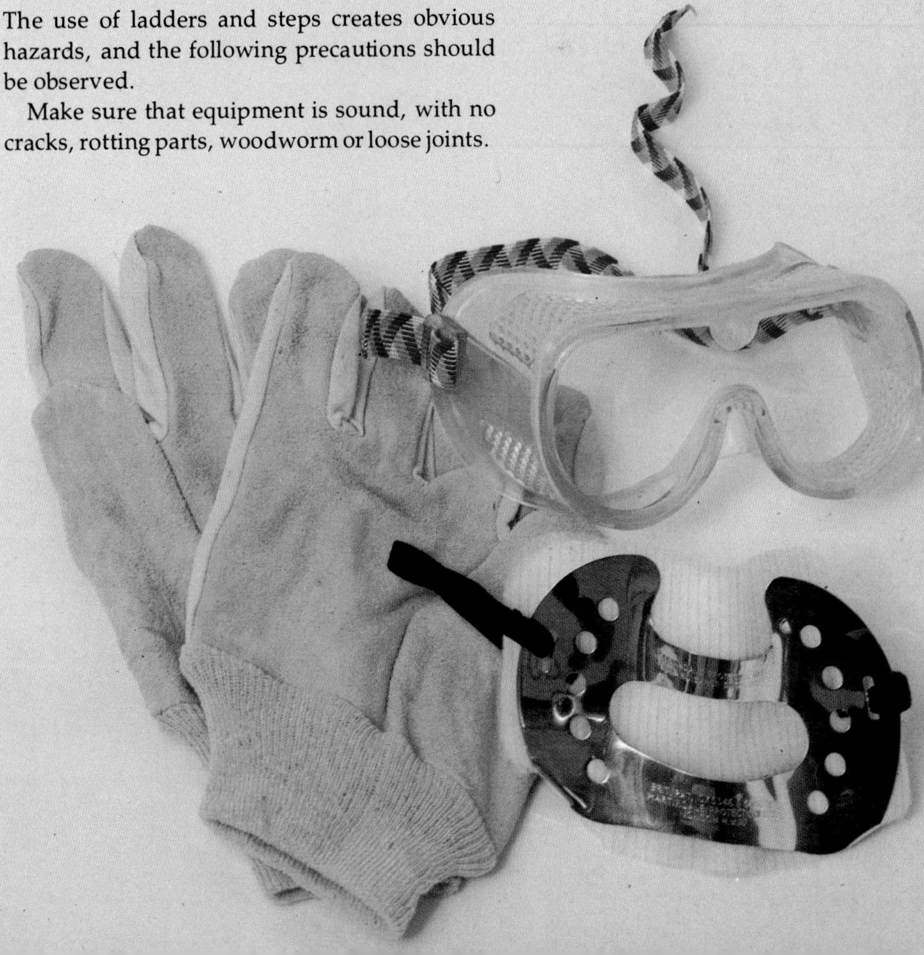

Steps should be fully open when in use. They must not rock; on an uneven surface use wood blocks to keep the steps steady. Platform steps with a hand-hold are the wisest choice for anyone unsure of heights.

The chapter on Roofs (pages 48-53) contains safety hints for working at a height out of doors. Ideally, ladders should be placed on firm, non-slip, level ground. Put chocks under one leg if the ground is uneven. On soft ground stand the ladder on a wide board.

The base of the ladder should be placed 1 metre out from the wall for every 4 metres of height. Anchor the base by lashing it to a peg, or wedge it with a sandbag if the ground is hard.

An extension ladder must have at least a three-rung overlap between sections.

Tie the top of the ladder to a large screw eye fixed to the gutter fascia. Do not rest the top of the ladder against glass, slates or thin plastic or asbestos-cement guttering. If necessary fix a ladder-stay to the top of the ladder to deal with a wide overhang. Never over-reach to one side while working on a ladder.

Always use crawling boards when working on a roof; like ladders, these can be hired. A scaffold tower should be used when working with crawling boards, but if a ladder is used there must be at least two rungs above gutter level to allow you to transfer to the crawling boards.

Scaffold towers make ideal platforms for high work. Never exceed the manufacturer's recommendations for free-standing height (usually

RIGHT: *When working with sharp tools such as chisels, always keep both hands and your body behind the cutting edge.*
BELOW: *On uneven floors, use a packing piece under the stepladder foot to prevent rocking.*
BELOW RIGHT: *If you feel unsafe on standard steps, choose those which have a special support rail.*

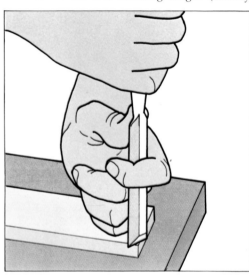

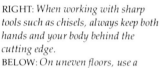

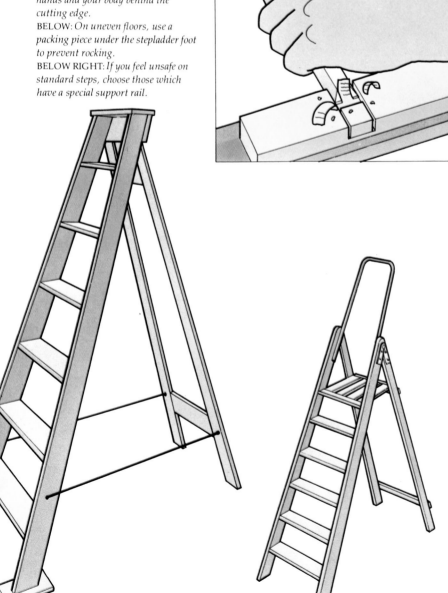

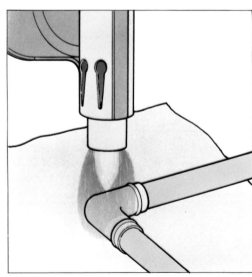

ABOVE: *When you are working with a blowlamp, place a non-flammable sheet such as a fire-blanket behind the surface you are working on.*

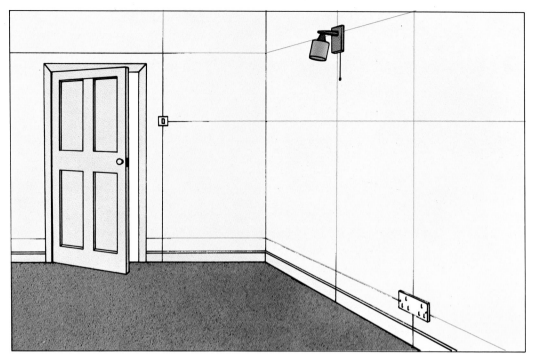

four times the minimum base dimension) without tying the tower to a secure part of the building. Use a spirit level to check that the tower is erected vertically. Fit the recommended number of diagonal braces and always fit guard rails at the top.

Working with electricity

Always disconnect electrical equipment from the power supply before inspecting or working on it. Unplug appliances. Switch off at the main fuse box before working on equipment wired to the mains, such as light switches or socket outlets.

If you are not sure about safety, consult a qualified electrician. Attempt only those electrical repair jobs described in this book. They have been selected with safety in mind.

Ensure that wires are connected to the correct terminal posts and learn the new wiring colour codes:

Green and yellow : earth
Brown   : live
Blue   : neutral

All equipment must be earthed, unless it is labelled as double-insulated and is marked with a square within a square. Consult an electrician if you are uncertain.

Safety with gas

See Emergency repairs, page 91.

Danger from fire

Exercise caution when using blowtorches or blowlamps. Never use a blowlamp near the eaves of a house; it can cause a fire in the roof space. When using a blowtorch to make capillary soldered joints in plumbing, place an asbestos blanket or sheet of soft asbestos (not asbestos cement) behind the joint if it is near to a wooden surface.

Poisonous Substances

These *must* be kept locked and out of reach of children. Make sure all containers are correctly labelled. Do not store poisonous substances in old soft drink bottles.

Cutting tools

Take particular care to ensure that the cutting direction is away from your body and fingers. Keep onlookers clear from the working area. When using a chisel keep the tool sharp and work with both hands on the tool.

When using power saws, *always* unplug before making adjustments to the tool. Keep fingers and clothing well away from the blade when it is in use. Make sure the guard is working properly.

Before drilling or cutting into walls check that no pipes or electric cables are below the surface. These will probably run vertically or horizontally in the wall and are most likely to be immediately above, below or beside electrical fittings or plumbing fixtures.

Chemicals

Follow the manufacturer's instructions. Work in a well ventilated place if fumes are harmful, as with some adhesives. Do not smoke or use electrical equipment if the chemical gives off a flammable vapour. Store carefully, out of the reach of children.

Lifting weights

When lifting heavy objects keep the legs bent and the back straight. Get someone to help you if possible.

Emergency repairs

Broken windows and faults in the main services of water, electricity and gas are the usual household emergencies which need immediate repair. In some cases the repair will be permanent, but in others it will be a temporary measure.

Broken window panes

If security is a problem, replace the glass immediately, see Replacing broken glass, page 25.

A small pane can be replaced temporarily with a sheet of clear polythene, hardboard or even cardboard pinned to the frame or fixed with sticky tape. Waterproof mastic tape can be stuck over bad cracks.

A large broken pane can also be covered with polythene, but this must be reinforced with timber battens tacked to the edges (*see diagram 1*). Start at the top, wrapping the polythene around a batten tacked to the top of the window frame (*see diagram 2*). Wrap the bottom edge of the plastic around a similar batten fixed to the sill so the plastic is taut. Secure the sides with two more battens placed over the plastic sheet (*see diagram 3*).

Plumbing emergencies

Water leaks often cause serious damage to walls, ceilings and floors. If the leak is coming from a pipe you can see, turn off the water supply at the stop valve nearest to the leak.

If the leak is obviously in the roof space, turn off the water supply where it enters the house (*see diagram 4*). This is usually a rising main with a tap set in the pipe just above the floor, and is normally in the vicinity of the kitchen sink.

Open every tap in the house to drain the cold water storage cistern (or tank) and all pipes as quickly as possible. While the pipes are draining turn off gas or oil boilers, water heaters, and rake out solid fuel boilers.

The next step is to find the cause of the leak. Look for pipes that have burst or split, pipework joints that have come apart, or storage cisterns that have rusted holes or split seams. When you have discovered the problem, turn to the Plumbing chapter, page 42, to see how to fix it.

If water starts to pour from the overflow pipe of a water storage cistern or lavatory cistern, turn off the supply immediately or the cistern may overflow.

A steady drip from the overflow pipe is more likely to be caused by a faulty ball valve washer, see page 45.

If a sink, basin or bath is blocked, check that the outside waste gully is not blocked by leaves. If the gulley is clear the cause is probably a build up of solids in the waste pipe. Run some water into the sink, cover the overflow with a wet cloth and work a rubber plunger up and down over the waste outlet.

If this does not clear the blockage put a bowl under the waste trap U-bend and unscrew the stopper in the bend (*see diagram 5*). Use a hooked wire to pull out debris. Some plastic traps have a bottle with a base that can be unscrewed to clear blockages (*see diagram 6*), or the entire bend may be removed to clear debris.

Electrical emergencies

Sudden electrical failure is usually caused by the cut out of a fuse, or, in rare cases, a circuit breaker.

BELOW: *Three stages of an emergency repair for a broken window. Polythene sheeting is tacked to battens fixed around the main window frame.*

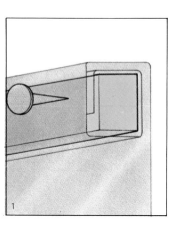

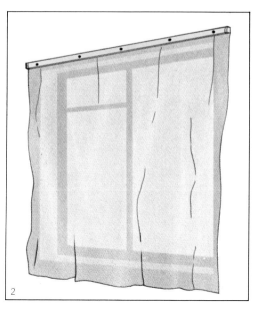

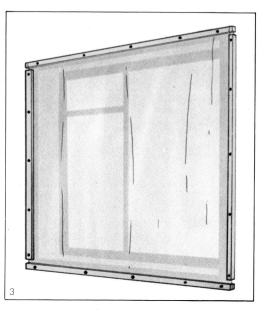

If one appliance fails, test the socket outlet by plugging in another appliance. Then check the plug fuse. Loosen the retaining screw of the plug and remove the cover to reach the fuse. Test the fuse using a battery torch. Fit a new 3-amp fuse for lights or appliances rated up to 720 watts or a 13-amp fuse for appliances rated between 721 and 3,000 watts.

When several lights or a number of socket outlets fail, a fuse or circuit breaker at the main fuse box has blown. Turn off the power at the main switch and check the fuses (see Electrical repairs, page 37). If you suspect that the fuse has blown because of a faulty appliance, unplug it before turning on the current at the main switch. Circuit breakers are reset by pressing the button or switch.

If the fault cannot be traced, or if every light and electrical appliance in the house has failed, check that there is not a general power cut, then call in the electricity board to check the main sealed fuse which protects their meter.

Gas emergencies

If there is a strong smell of gas, turn off the main gas tap near the meter (*see diagram 7*). The tap spindle has a deep line across it and the gas is off when this line is at right angles to the pipe. The gas tap handle is usually at right angles to the gas pipe when the gas is off, but the spindle line is a more reliable guide (*see diagram 8*).

Extinguish any naked flames and call the gas board. Open all windows and wait for the smell of gas to clear before touching any electrical switches.

If the smell of gas is slight a pilot light may have gone out. Clear the gas as detailed above and relight the pilot light or burner. If the smell recurs there is probably a slight leak. Turn off the gas at the main tap and call the gas board.

If you suspect a joint of a slight leak, check it by dripping a mixture of equal parts water and washing-up liquid on to the joint. If gas is escaping, bubbles will form. Call in the gas board to repair the joint.

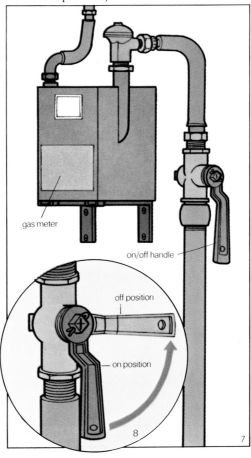

gas meter

on/off handle

off position

on position

8

7

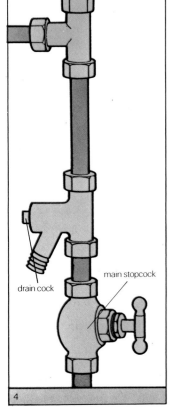

drain cock

main stopcock

4

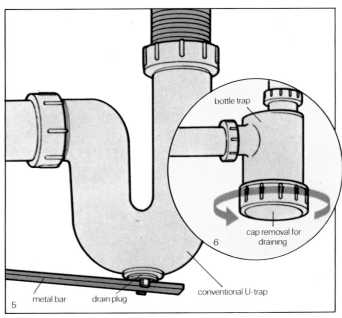

bottle trap

cap removal for draining

conventional U-trap

6

metal bar

drain plug

5

FAR LEFT: *When problems occur in the plumbing system, always turn off the main supply stopcock before starting a repair.*
ABOVE: *If you need to turn off the gas supply, you'll find the turn off point near the meter in the feed pipe.*
LEFT: *Blocked waste pipes can often be cleared by removing matter from the trap.*

Maintenance checks

Many emergency repairs, and indeed many routine repair jobs, can be avoided by regular maintenance checks. It would be useful if you could set up your own routine. Make checklists which cover items that need looking at frequently, and those which you can examine every year or half year.

Plumbing Checks

Stop-cocks can jam through disuse. Two or three times a year they should be fully closed (turn clockwise), then opened again. A stiff handle should ease off after a couple of operations.

If the handle will not turn readily, place an adjustable spanner over the handle and apply moderate pressure. If this does not work, loosen the gland nut, hook out the gland packing and trickle some graphited penetrating oil down the spindle. Leave for 24 hours (with a bucket to catch any drips from the spindle) and try the handle again. If it remains rigid, heat the headgear with a blowlamp.

A tap which continues to drip after being shut down requires a new washer. The same is true if the handle needs excessive pressure to stop a drip (see Plumbing repairs, page 43).

If a new washer does not cure a dripping tap the seating may be worn and should be replaced with a Full Stop combined washer and nylon seating set.

If water leaks from between the spindle and the shield when a tap is turned on, take off the handle and shield and give the gland nut about ¼ turn. Check that the leak has stopped and that the tap is not too stiff to turn. If the leak persists, the gland must be repacked, see Plumbing repairs, page 45.

Electrical checks

Warning: **Never** work on live equipment. When working on an electrical appliance always remove the plug from the socket outlet. When working on permanently wired equipment, such as a light flex, switch off the electricity supply at the main switch on the consumer unit. Isolate the relevant circuit by removing the appropriate fuse. Check terminals with mains tester screwdriver.

Once a year check the plugs on all electrical appliances. Terminals can work loose and cause sparking which could start a fire. Take off the plug cover and check that the wires are well anchored in the terminals with no fraying wires protruding from the connections. Make sure the insulation is sound and that the outer insulation on the flex is well anchored in the clamp at the mouth of the plug. If braided flex is fraying around the fabric edges, wrap the flex with mastic adhesive tape.

Check along the entire length of the flexes of all appliances, and replace any that show signs of cuts or wear. Electric iron flex is particularly prone to wear.

Lighting flexes should be checked and replaced from time to time because of the heat generated by electric light bulbs. The insulation can become brittle and crack, particularly at the end near the bulb-holder (see Electrical repairs, page 39).

Extractor fans should be cleaned regularly and oiled according to the manufacturer's instructions.

Checks on doors and windows

Oil hinges, locks and catches occasionally and dismantle locks for oiling. Check draught excluders and replace if necessary. Wipe curtain tracks with a damp cloth soaked in washing-up liquid and apply silicone-base polish where the gliders will slide.

Checks on walls and paintwork

Refix loose and torn wallpaper and repair chipped paintwork as soon as the damage is seen (see Interior walls pages 20-23).

Examine wall fixings, like shelf brackets, to make sure they are secure. If loose, fit a larger wall plug and longer screw. If the hole is over-size or distorted, fill the hole with an asbestos compound filler and replace the screw.

Central heating checks

Keep the boiler clean. Close down the boiler, remove the cover and use a vacuum cleaner to remove fluff from the interior. Clean air vents. With solid fuel boilers clean the flue once a year. Boiler adjustments and other maintenance work should be carried out only by a qualified heating engineer.

If the circulating pump becomes noisy and does not circulate water properly, there may be an air lock. Open the vent valve as shown in the operating instructions or call a heating engineer.

If a radiator is not heating properly, turn the key in the air valve at the top of the radiator to clear the air.

With an oil-fired system, keep the oil storage tank well painted to prevent the metal rusting. Once a year drain off sludge and water from the drain cock, and remove and clean the oil filter in the supply pipe. Make sure the tank vent pipe is clear of dirt and that the filler pipe cap is easy to turn.

OPPOSITE: Regular checks on frequently used items of electrical equipment ensure that they do not become dangerous.

AC This stands for alternating current, as opposed to direct current (DC).

Airbrick This looks like an ordinary brick, but contains small round holes, or a small grating. It will be set low down in an outside wall, and its purpose is to ventilate wooden ground floors, and prevent dampness caused by condensation.

Amps Short for amperes. A unit of measurement for electric current.

Arris This is the sharp corner or edge where two surfaces meet; you may come across this term in brickwork or masonry, where the corners of bricks and stones are known as *arrises*.

Balusters These are the upright sections that support the hand-rail on a staircase.

Beading is a small strip of moulding, made of timber or plastic, often used to finish off work.

Bearer Bearers provide *horizontal* support; this term is often used for small timber sections supporting shelves, sinks, cupboards and so on.

Bevel An angled or sloping edge, as for example in a bevelled mirror.

Bitumen A tar-like waterproof material which is used for making asphalt, roofing felts, and damp-courses.

Bolster Bricklayer's chisel.

Breeze blocks Large building blocks of precast clinker concrete.

Burning-off A method of removing paint by using a blowlamp to soften and blister the paint covering, which can then be scraped away.

Butt-joining Joining two surfaces together without any overlap; it is the kind of join you make when hanging wallpaper.

Cavity wall A wall made in a double layer with a gap in the middle, tie-irons or cavity ties hold the two walls together at intervals.

Centres Carpentry or fixing instructions will often tell you to fix things 'at x centres'. This means make your fixings at intervals of whatever x is.

Chamfer This is a carpentry term, describing where two surfaces meet at right angles, and the edge is shaved away to form an angled corner.

Channel This simply means a groove, either cut into a material or fixed onto it as a 'U' shaped section.

Chase or chasing A channel or groove cut out to receive a pipe or wiring, for example.

Circuit breakers are fitted to fuse boxes in some houses, instead of fuses, as a protection against overloading.

Cisterns are tanks for water, either for storage or for flushing.

Cladding Any material used to face a building or structure.

Conduit The protective casing for electric cables.

Coping is the brick or stone used to finish off the top of a wall.

Cove A moulding which fits into the angle between the top of the wall and the ceiling — useful for concealing cracks.

Cramp An alternative for *clamp*.

Curtain wall This is a term you may meet in modern architecture for a non-loadbearing (non-structural) wall.

Dado The lower part of an inside wall, with a different decorative finish from the rest.

Damp-proof course (d.p.c.) The layer at a bottom of a wall that stops the progress of damp. It can commonly be made of slate, lead, bitumen, copper or zinc.

Damp-proof membrane A damp-proof layer applied to floors to check the penetration of damp.

Dowel A small piece of wood (or sometimes metal) shaped like a cylinder, and used for fixing two pieces of material firmly together.

Dry rot Wood decay caused by fungus.

Earthed When an appliance is earthed, it is in effect connected for safety reasons to the mass of the earth. The earth wire in a flex is coloured yellow and green, the live is coloured brown (previously red) and the neutral is coloured blue (previously black).

Eaves The lowest overhanging part of a sloping roof.

Elbows are pipe fittings for connecting two lengths of pipe to each other at various angles, e.g. 90°, 135°.

Fascia board Length of timber fixed vertically at the lowest end of rafters or spars.

Feather edge Boards cut to a very thin wedge shape.

Female fitting Plumbing term for a pipe fitting which has a socket, plain or threaded, into which a tube or 'male' fitting can be inserted.

Fillet A term used in joinery for a small, thin strip of wood.

Floor joists Structural or bearing timbers suspended between supporting walls on which floorboards are laid.

Flush To finish off flush is to finish off level or flat.

Galvanized When steel is galvanized, it has been coated with zinc to prevent rust.

Gauge A standard of measure for the thickness of items such as sheet metal, wire, and screws.

Gland A sealing ring around the stem of a tap, valve or fitting. Glands prevent leaking and are generally adjustable.

Glasspaper is the correct term for sandpaper available in coarse, medium and fine grades for different applications.

Glazing beads are strips of timber used with putty to hold glass within a frame.

Grain This describes the way the fibres of wood run.

Grout or grouting is a waterproof cement-based paste used for filling in gaps between ceramic tiles; conveniently available ready-mixed.

Hardcore Broken brick, stone or rubble used as a base for floors, pavings and roads.

Hardwood Simply means timber from any deciduous tree, and even includes balsa wood.

Hips The line where two sloping edges of a roof meet.

Inspection chamber Commonly called a manhole. A way of getting down to an underground drainage system.

Jamb The vertical face inside a door or window opening.

Joist Timber or steel beam supporting a floor or ceiling. An r.s.j. (rolled steel joist) is used to support a ceiling when a structural wall has been removed.

Jubilee clips Handy bands of metal which can be tightened by means of a metal screw to fit rubber hose or piping firmly onto taps.

Kerf The cut made by a saw.

Key To key a surface is to roughen it so that another material can adhere properly.

Kilowatt A unit of electricity equal to 1,000 watts.

Kilowatt hour The amount of electricity used by an appliance is measured in kWh; this is 1,000W used for one hour.

Lagging The insulating material which is wrapped around pipes and tanks to prevent them from freezing. Hot water tanks should also be lagged as an economy measure.

Lap joint Wallpaper joint with a slight overlap (c.f. butt joint).

Lintel The stone, timber or reinforced concrete beam spanning an opening such as a door or window.

Load-bearing wall A wall which is carrying the weight of the structure above it, which could be another storey, or the roof.

Making good Getting rid of surface defects before painting or papering.

Masking out Covering up a surface (e.g. with adhesive tape) to prevent paint from adhering.

Mitre A 45° diagonal join between two right-angled surfaces. Usually cut with the aid of a mitre block.

Mortise A hole, usually rectangular in shape. which has been cut out of a piece of wood to take a fitting.

Newel The main supporting post for stairs and banisters.

Nipple A small valve which when opened with a key allows air to escape from a system.

Nosing The overhanging part of a stair tread.

Ogee A moulding shape, frequently used to describe a kind of gutter.

Oilstone A fine-grained stone used with a lubricant for sharpening tools.

Olive/compression ring A small copper or brass ring used in non-manipulative compression fittings.

P.a.r. An old-fashioned term standing for 'planed all round'. Prepared, or planed timber, will be slightly smaller, say 3mm (1/8in), than its stated size.

Pilot hole A hole drilled to make passage easier for the subsequent screw.

Pointing The mortar joints between brickwork; re-pointing involves raking out the old, soft mortar and re-filling the joints with mortar mix.

Quarry tiles Durable clay floor tiles, of a reddish colour.

Quoin The external corner of a wall.

Rebate A rectangular recess or step cut along an edge of a piece of wood.

Rendering A layer of cement mortar applied as a protective coating to outside brickwork.

Reveal The side of a window or door opening.

Ring main An electrical circuit arranged in the form of a ring.

Riser The vertical part of a step.

Screed A thin layer of plaster on a wall, or a thin layer of concrete applied to level a floor.

Scribing Marking a cutting line, usually with a knife or some other sharp instrument.

Shake A fault in a piece of timber, usually a split or a crack.

Soffit This describes the *underside* of an architectural feature. The soffit board, for example, is the horizontal board fixed to the underside of overhanging rafters.

Spur A branch cable from a ring circuit.

Stile The upright at the edge of wooden framing.

Stop cock The valve on a pipe which allows you to turn off the water supply.

Stretcher A brick laid with its long sides in line with the face of the wall.

String The timber side of a staircase which supports the steps.

Strippers Various proprietary mixtures of chemical solvents which can be applied to remove old paintwork.

Stucco A coat of fine plaster on a wall or ceiling.

Studs These are the uprights in a partition. A stud partition is constructed on a timber framework or skeleton.

Template A wood or metal pattern used as a guide for marking out a shape before cutting.

Thermal capacity The amount of heat a substance will absorb and store.

Tolerance The agreed amounts by which sizes may differ from standard sizes, to allow for imperfections in cutting etc.

Traps Sinks, WCs and gullies all have traps to seal off smells coming from the drains.

Turpentine substitute is white spirit.

Veneer Very thin sheets of decorative timber.

Volts (V) The unit for measuring the pressure or force which causes an electric current to flow in a circuit.

Water hammer Knocking sound occurring when a pipe is turned off quickly.

Wet-and-dry-paper Waterproof abrasive papers that can be used wet for rubbing down paintwork, the water acting as a lubricant.

Index

Acknowledgements

The publishers would like to thank the following organisations and individuals for their kind permission to reproduce the photographs in this book:
Paul Brierley: 67; Natural History Photographic Agency (Stephen Dalton): 75 top and below, 77 above right and left, centre; Rentokil Limited: 72, 73, 74, 75 above, centre and bottom, 77 top, below left and right.
Special photography: John Cook/Whitecross Studio: 1-9, 16-17, 26-27, 34, 48-49, 54, 56, 58-59, 70, 78-79, 80-87, 93.

Jacket photography: Robert Golden.

Illustrations by Terry Allen Design Limited/Lyn Brooks, Roger Courthold, Robert Stoneman.

The publishers would also like to thank the following for kindly lending their products to be used for photography:
E. Amette & Co. Ltd. Pentoville Road, London N.1; Chandlers Woodshops, New Kings Road, London S.W.6; Waterford Road Garden Centre, London S.W.6.

Contributing editors: John McGowan and Roger duBern of Do it Yourself Magazine.

PDO 81-842

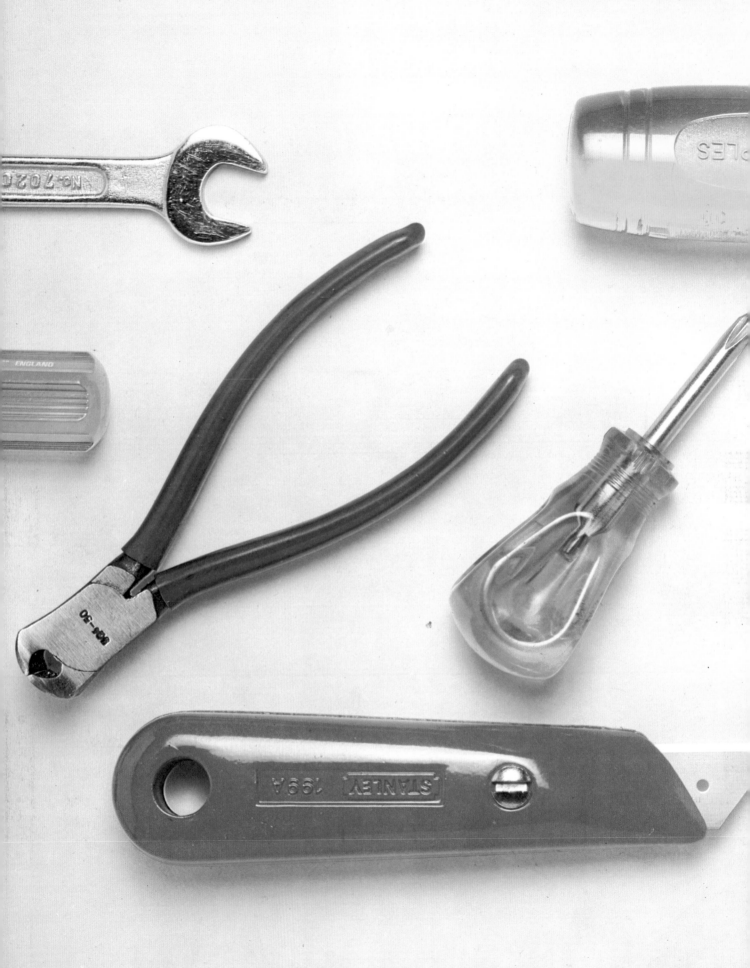